FINISH COLLEGE IN HIGH SCHOOL

The Family Guide to a
DEBT-FREE DEGREE
with Dual Enrollment

SHELLEY BRANINE

Finish College in High School
The Family Guide to a Debt-Free Degree with Dual Enrollment
by Shelley Branine

1. EDU015000   EDUCATION / Schools / Levels / Higher
2. BUS050030   BUSINESS & ECONOMICS / Personal Finance /
Money Management
3. EDU025000   EDUCATION / Schools / Levels / Secondary

ISBN: (paperback) 979-8-88636-069-1
ISBN: (ebook) 979-8-88636-070-7

Library of Congress Control Number: 2025925190

Cover design by Lewis Agrell

Printed in the United States of America

Authority Publishing
13389 Folsom Blvd #300-256
Folsom, CA 95630
800-877-1097
www.AuthorityPublishing.com

Dual enrollment is one of the most overlooked yet powerful ways families can dramatically cut college costs, and Shelley Branine makes it clear why it should be on every parent's radar. Having spent years helping students navigate the rising price of higher education and tracking college affordability and student loan policy, I can say her approach is one of the smartest and most effective tools parents have to avoid debt before it ever begins—yet far too few ever hear about it. This book gives families a clear, workable plan to earn college credit in high school, protect their finances, and shift a student's entire financial path before they ever step onto a traditional college campus. Grounded in real experience and practical guidance, it shows what's possible when families understand the system and use it as it was designed.

— **Robert Farrington**, America's Millennial Money Expert®, America's Student Loan Debt Expert™, and Founder of *The College Investor*

I strongly recommend this book to every ambitious high school student and their parents. Shelley Branine lays out an efficient, effective guidepath in these quickly changing times for giving our nation's kids the best start in life possible. She shows families how to avoid the growing minefield of hazards that are baked into the traditional path to getting a quality college degree. This country would be in a much better place if everyone took the advice laid out in this book!

— **Alan Collinge**, Founder of Student Loan Justice and Author of *The Student Loan Scam*

Shelley Branine's book is the missing piece of the college funding puzzle. I regularly work with hardworking parents who are concerned about high tuition costs and skyrocketing student debt. They don't want to sacrifice their retirement to put their children through college. This book on dual enrollment is a breath of fresh air, offering a solid financial strategy to build wealth rather than accumulate more debt.

— **Deb Meyer**, Founder of WorthyNest®, Author of *Redefining Family Wealth*, and host of the Beyond Budgets® podcast.

In *Finish College in High School*, Shelley Branine brings much needed attention to dual enrollment, an often overlooked but incredibly powerful pathway to a debt-free college education.

— **Andy Hill**, Host of Marriage Kids and Money and Author of *Own Your Time*

Early College High Schools ignite possibility—giving students the chance to earn college credit, build real confidence, and step boldly into their future long before graduation day. The impact is electric. And author Shelley Branine captures that energy brilliantly. Through her vibrant storytelling and unwavering passion for student success, she shines a spotlight on the life-changing power of Early College experiences. Her work doesn't just describe the transformation—it celebrates it, elevates it, and inspires others to join in creating these opportunities for every student.

— **Dr. Jill Gildea**, CEO - Colorado Early Colleges

Finish College in High School is one of the best-kept secrets out there—and it blew me away. Shelley Branine reveals a little-known path that allows families to save tens of thousands of dollars while helping teens earn a college degree debt-free. She shows that college doesn't have to drain savings or leave students buried in loans, especially for teens who feel bored or disengaged in traditional school. This book lays out a clear, proven roadmap that not only lowers the cost of college, but also helps students regain motivation, build confidence, and find a learning path that truly fits them. It's one of the smartest and most affordable approaches to college I've ever seen, and a must-read for any parent who wants their teen to thrive while graduating 100% debt-free.

— **Sheryl Gould**, Parent Educator, Founder of *Moms of Tweens and Teens*, and Author of *SOS! The Technology Guidebook for Parents of Tweens and Teens*

For Caitlyn and Karissa.
None of this would be possible without you.

CONTENTS

PREFACE

Warning: The information in this book has the potential to empower young people for the rest of their lives. Despite what they may say, many high schools, universities, and even certain government agencies do not want you to have access to this knowledge. However, before you dive in, keep in mind that for your kids to succeed, it may require a shift in mindset for the entire family.

First, it's important to recognize that eighteen- to twenty-five-year-olds face greater financial challenges than any other generation in history. Student loan debt is at an all-time high, totaling over $1.8 trillion, with the average loan balance exceeding $40,000.[1] College tuition prices are skyrocketing, having outpaced inflation by nearly 500%. Housing prices are also rapidly increasing, and in less than a decade, homeownership among young adults declined by nearly 10%.[2] In addition, wages for young adults have not kept pace with the cost of living, and real income has largely remained flat over the last two decades, even as housing and education costs have soared.[3] At the same time, student loans are arguably the most risky and potentially devastating form of debt in U.S. history, yet we provide them to our young adults in unlimited amounts as if they were candy.[4]

Now more than ever, parents must protect their kids from financial disaster and earning college credits while in high school is a powerful option toward building a strong financial foundation. By taking advantage of these opportunities, your family can save thousands of dollars while giving your child a competitive edge in an increasingly challenging job market. This book will help you maximize the number of free college credits your child can earn while in high school. But first, let me share why our family chose this unconventional approach to education.

Our two daughters graduated college a week before finishing high school. One walked the graduation stage in May of 2021, and the other finished in May of 2023. Because they were technically still high school students, almost every penny of their associate degrees was paid for by the state of Colorado, allowing them to start their bachelor's degrees with two years of college already completed. They were typical high school students. They don't have exceptionally high IQs; in fact, one has a disability and has always required accommodations and extra support with academics. They also did not miss out on the "high school experience." They participated in high school—and even college-level—sports, homecoming, prom, and one served as student council president. While we have done our best to encourage a strong work ethic, please keep in mind that we do not consider either of our girls overachievers. We simply recognized a hidden opportunity in the Colorado school system and took advantage of it, and most states offer similar options.

Before I explain how our girls accomplished this, let me share why we chose this untraditional path in education. In 1997, my husband, Erik, and I graduated from a private religious college with a combined student loan debt of $50,000. When we entered college at 18 years old, we attended a financial aid meeting where the repercussions of debt were briefly and vaguely discussed, but no one mentioned it again. No family member, school official, clergyman or woman, or anyone else in authority ever helped us understand the importance of financial planning, nor did they suggest alternative methods for paying for college.

Upon graduation, the weight of $50,000 in debt was devastating. We felt defeated even before we began our professional lives. In addition, we had no idea how to manage that level of debt. We graduated with degrees that led to low-paying jobs—one as a teacher and the other as a radio broadcaster—and we chose to live in Colorado, a state with one of the highest costs of living. But those are topics for another time. It took us years to overcome that amount of debt on such low salaries, and early on, we vowed that our children would not make the same mistakes we made. And so far, they haven't.

Sadly, today, over 20 years later, the amount of student loan debt is rapidly increasing, with no reasonable solutions available to borrowers. As a result, I am committed to using the knowledge I've gained from my daughters' experiences, along with the insights I've gathered from working with other kids and sharing it with any families who are open to it. I believe that starting adulthood debt-free gives young adults the upper hand and empowers them to achieve much more than they otherwise could. However, keep in mind that unless a large college fund has been established, the journey may require your family to go against the flow, raise a few eyebrows, do things that others don't understand, and possibly face criticism. But eventually, the critics will wish they had followed your lead. Both of my daughters will graduate from a four-year university 100% debt-free, and I want the same for all young adults!

"First, they make fun of you. Then they say you're crazy. And then they ask you how you did it." Codie Sanchez

CHAPTER 1:
WHY CONSIDER DUAL ENROLLMENT?

After graduating from college, I briefly worked in the admissions department at my university, where I met countless students entering college with credits paid for by their school districts. Since my husband, Erik, and I had $50,000 in combined student loan debt, I couldn't help but feel envious. I had entered college four years earlier with a less-than-stellar GPA, which meant that I was eligible for very few scholarships, and as a result, most of my education was funded by loans. I couldn't believe that earning free college credits in high school was even an option. I also recalled my dislike for traditional high school and realized that dual enrollment would have been a better fit for me. For this reason, I promised myself that, when I had kids, I would make sure they understood the value of earning college credits while still in high school. As a result of our family's journey, I have also had the privilege of getting to know many other young people and helping them take advantage of similar opportunities.

Finish College in High School is a labor of love, inspired by my family's journey through dual enrollment. My mission is to empower parents and students who want to take advantage of earning college credits while still in high school. The truth is that, aside from student loans, there is limited funding available to help young people finance college, while tuition prices are rapidly increasing. According to Mike Rowe, podcaster and creator of the show *Dirty Jobs*, "You can't find anything in the last 50 years that has gotten more expensive more rapidly than a college degree, not food, energy, healthcare, or even real estate. It has outpaced inflation by about 500%." At the same time, scholarships are minimal and extremely competitive, and the full-ride scholarship has become an urban legend, almost nonexistent.

Aside from awards for the rare star athlete or child prodigy, to my knowledge, there is only one option available that guarantees free college tuition for anyone who wants it: earning college credit while in high school, also known as *dual enrollment*. My desire is to help anyone who might feel intimidated, unsure, afraid of missing out, fearful of the unknown, or concerned about being "weird," as well as those who had no idea that these types of programs even exist.

The truth is that young people and their parents are being coerced into accumulating overwhelming debt to pay for college. They are sold lies such as students should attend their dream college regardless of cost; bright students always receive full scholarships; student loans are not a big deal and loan forgiveness is readily available; AP and IB programs offer the most promising future; the neighborhood school is always the best option for your kids; and students who attend college while in high school will miss out on the "high school experience," among many others. Millions of students believed these lies and felt they had no choice but to take out student loans. As a result, they now feel blindsided by the loan industry, which has completely devastated their lives.

I want to help you protect your kids from this type of devastation. Dual enrollment offers guaranteed free money for tuition and allows families to avoid accumulating massive amounts of student loan debt. This book is designed to provide step-by-step guidance and help you make the most of this valuable resource. You can read it from beginning to end or explore various chapters as needed.

It is also meant to accompany my website, FinishCollegeinHighSchool.com, which was created for parents, grandparents, or guardians considering dual enrollment for their kids, to ease their concerns and encourage them to give it a try. This guide will delve deeper and provide everything you need to know to ensure your child's success in earning college credits while in high school.

College is not easy, and it will require work. However, the substantial rewards are worth the effort. Please keep this guide close by throughout your journey and refer to it as challenges arise. Remember, there is a way over, under, or around any hurdle you encounter. I want to help you succeed; I want to be your cheerleader, encouraging you to persevere, fight the fight, and eventually cross the finish line. Whether your child earns a degree while in high school or simply explores various options, I am here to help you make the most of every opportunity available, while also saving thousands of dollars on a college education. Thank you for allowing me to be a part of your journey. I am excited for the adventure that lies ahead.

CHAPTER 2:
IS DUAL ENROLLMENT A REALISTIC OPTION FOR YOUR FAMILY?

While dual enrollment is gradually gaining popularity among high schoolers, it is still widely misunderstood by or unknown to many families. As a result, there are few resources available to help parents and guardians guide their children through the process. My goal is to provide the information and support needed to help your child succeed in taking college classes while still in high school.

I firmly believe that with the right support and practical insights, any student can succeed in dual enrollment, even if they decide after a few courses that college isn't the right path for them (I discuss this more in Chapter 5). In fact, after taking college courses, they might realize they'd prefer to learn a trade or pursue a career that doesn't require a college degree. What better time to discover this than while still in high school, when they don't have to pay for tuition?

As you read our story, I'll share some of the mistakes we made—though there were many more. Most of the successes you'll read about came from figuring things out after doing them the wrong way or wasting too much time. My goal is to share the knowledge we gained from those mistakes to help you save time and avoid common setbacks.

When considering whether dual enrollment is a realistic option for your family, it's important to acknowledge the time commitment required. My daughters, for example, actually preferred the college schedule to the high school one. They loved attending classes a few days a week for just a few hours, as opposed to a full day of high school followed by an evening of homework. The college schedule gave them more flexibility to study or work a part-time job during the day, leaving more time for socializing. However, some students may struggle with this flexibility and might need more structure. If that's the case, I recommend finding a program that brings college classes to the high school. I will discuss different types of dual enrollment programs in the next Chapter.

High schoolers who struggle with motivation or tend to be noncompliant may not initially thrive in college classes. However, they might also excel once they experience the freedom, flexibility, and academic rigor that college offers. I can personally relate to this. During high school, I was unmotivated, struggled with the traditional school environment, and didn't succeed in many of my classes. Yet, after graduating, I discovered a passion for college coursework and became a successful student almost overnight. Many kids who face similar challenges in high school may find that they thrive in a college setting, which is why dual enrollment could be a better fit for some.

My Story:
Struggling in High School, Thriving in College

When I was a high school senior, my English teacher pulled me aside after class. "Shelley, you are a terrible student," she began, her tone painfully serious. "But," she continued, "I actually think you could be really successful in college." She was right about both. I barely made it out of high school with a 2.0 GPA, but in my first semester of college, I earned a 4.0.

To me, college wasn't "more school"; it was a completely different environment. I had more freedom, fewer busywork assignments, and professors who treated me like an adult. For the first time, I felt respected, motivated, and in control of my own learning. That change made all the difference.

That's why I remind families that struggling in high school doesn't mean a student won't succeed in college. Sometimes, the environment is the problem, and dual enrollment allows students to test that fit early, without the financial risk.

For more information on students who struggle in high school but thrive in college, see my blog post "Myth: Struggles in High School Will Also Persist in College" on FinishCollegeinHighSchool.com.

That said, it's also possible that some students may need a bit more time to mature before taking on college-level coursework. In such cases, waiting a semester or even a year could make all the difference.

This was the case with our oldest, Caitlyn. We didn't seriously consider college classes until she was nearing the end of tenth grade. She had many special needs throughout elementary and middle school, which I discuss more in Chapter 9. However, by the end of tenth grade, she had matured significantly and came to us, saying that she was considering dual enrollment.

You may also be wondering about the time commitment for you as a parent. In the beginning, your kids will probably need more support during their first few college classes, but over time, they should be able to take on more responsibility as they gain confidence. During those early classes, we supported our girls for about an hour (give or take) a few evenings each week. Erik helped with math and science, while I assisted with English and social sciences. However, keep in mind that most colleges offer tutoring and writing centers, so if you're not confident in certain subjects, there's no need to worry; your kids can take full advantage of these resources instead.

Additionally, Erik and I both worked full-time while the girls were participating in dual enrollment, and I had a job that required weekly travel. Despite this, we found supporting our kids through dual enrollment to be manageable. We simply had to plan ahead and schedule the times we would help.

However, if this level of commitment feels unmanageable, keep in mind that some states offer dual enrollment schools that function like traditional high schools but also bring college professors to campus. These schools, often called early colleges, typically have processes in place, such as onsite tutoring and staff dedicated to ensuring students' success in college courses. In this case, you wouldn't need to provide as much support, since the school offers the resources and guidance necessary for your kids to succeed.

I want to be transparent and acknowledge upfront that organization and task management come fairly naturally to me. After all, I was the "annoying" parent who joked that leading a Girl Scout troop was a piece of cake, while other moms stood behind me, rolling their eyes. That said, I don't want you to feel that you need to have the same strengths to be successful. I certainly don't have it all figured out, and there were plenty of times when I struggled to support my kids through dual enrollment. I share this to offer some perspective, not to suggest that you need to follow our exact approach.

My goal is simply to share what we've learned, hoping it will make your journey easier. Take what resonates with you, and feel free to disregard the rest. Ultimately, the most important goal is for your kids to earn as many college credits as possible while saving the most money. You have your own unique strengths, so feel free to use our ideas and experiences to create a plan that works best for your family.

To Recap:

1. Any student can succeed in dual enrollment, even if they just take a few classes and determine that college is not the right fit for them.
2. Some students may need a year or two to mature before they're ready for dual enrollment. However, it can also be a great option for students who seem unmotivated or noncompliant, as the flexibility and increased academic challenge may be exactly what they need.
3. You may need to schedule time to support your kids with their classes. However, if that seems unmanageable, colleges provide help through tutoring and writing centers.
4. If you feel you can't support your child adequately, consider a dual enrollment high school or early college that brings college classes to the campus, with onsite tutoring and staff dedicated to ensuring your child succeeds.
5. Use our ideas and experiences to create a unique plan that works best for your family, and feel free to disregard what doesn't resonate with you.

As you consider college classes for your high schooler, remember that you don't need to have a perfect plan or be fully organized from the start. The journey will involve learning and adjustments along the way, and that's okay. What matters most is that you remain flexible, support your kids, and stay focused on the goal of earning as many free college credits as possible.

CHAPTER 3:
FINDING THE RIGHT DUAL ENROLLMENT PROGRAM FOR YOUR FAMILY AND OVERCOMING INFORMATION BARRIERS

Most states offer multiple ways for students to earn college credits while in high school, but families often need to know where to look. I strongly believe that many public schools are reluctant to lose students to dual enrollment programs, and I explain my reasoning in Chapter 13. As a result, finding these options may require some effort.

It's important to note that states use varying terminology when referring to high school students earning college credit. The most widely used term for these programs is dual enrollment, so for simplicity, I will also refer to them as such. However, some states use other terms, such as dual credit, concurrent enrollment, and early college, among others. While these terms are largely interchangeable, the terminology may vary by state, and there are also differences in how the programs are implemented. These types of academic tracks allow high school students to enroll in college courses, which may be offered at a local college, online, or sometimes taught by college professors on the high school campus.

College Credit in High School:
Know the Terms

Students in nearly every U.S. state can earn college credit while still in high school. The names of these programs vary, and families may see them referred to as dual enrollment, dual credit, concurrent enrollment, concurrent education, or early college.

No matter the terminology, the goal is the same: to allow high school students to take college-level courses that count toward both high school and college graduation. These classes may be taught by professors on the high school campus, online, or at a local college. In most cases, tuition is covered by the school, district, or state, and some programs even cover books and fees.

Dual enrollment is the most common term, which is why I use it throughout this book, but families should remember that each state uses its own terminology and has its own rules.

For more information on the various programs, see my blog post "Dual Enrollment, AP, IB, and Early College: What Do These Terms Mean?" on FinishCollegeinHighSchool.com.

It's also worth clarifying that Advanced Placement (AP) and International Baccalaureate (IB) are not forms of dual enrollment. Unlike dual enrollment, which awards official college credit upon course completion, AP and IB require students to pass high-stakes final exams, and college credit is granted only if certain score thresholds are met—and even then, credit policies vary widely by college. I'll explore AP and IB in more detail in Chapter 13.

Since dual enrollment programs vary by state, I recommend starting with your school and district websites to see what's offered in your area. Just keep in mind that these can sometimes be vague and may not fully detail all the benefits available. For example, ours stated that only eleventh and twelfth graders could participate in dual enrollment and that students could take up to two classes each semester, but that turned out not to be the whole story.

From there, contact the guidance counselor at your local school and request as much information as possible about the dual enrollment program. While the details may still be somewhat vague, counselors often provide more insight than what's available online. In our case, the counselor clarified key eligibility requirements and course limits per semester, information not mentioned on the website, though she still didn't fully disclose all the available benefits.

I also recommend reaching out to the person or department responsible for dual enrollment in your district. Ask them to share everything you need to know about earning college credits while in high school, as you want to make the most of this opportunity. While our local district typically just redirected our questions back to the school, I've heard of district leaders who genuinely want to help parents and students find additional resources, so it's always worth asking.

You can also visit your state's department of education website to review their dual enrollment guidelines. We found that the state revealed information the district wasn't readily sharing and offered additional benefits for earning college credit in high school. We then took that information back to our district to see if they would allow students to take advantage of these additional opportunities.

Finally, it's most beneficial to call or email the dual enrollment representatives at your local community college. While the high school guidance counselor may be overworked, uninterested, or uninformed, community colleges welcome dual enrollment students because they bring in additional revenue. After speaking with our local community college, we discovered that the district would pay for not only one or two college courses, but up to three courses each semester, and students could start as early as ninth grade! This information was not readily shared by the district, which is why it can be helpful to reach out directly to the community college.

It took several months of calls and emails for us to uncover the full truth about the maximum benefits available to high school students. Ultimately, we learned that the state allows students to take an unlimited number of college courses, potentially earning a professional certificate, an associate degree, or, in some cases, even a bachelor's degree. It became clear that the district wasn't eager to share these details.

While we greatly appreciated the opportunity to earn college credits through dual enrollment at the neighborhood school, our experience there gradually became more challenging. As we sought approval for additional classes, we encountered increasing resistance, which I will discuss more in Chapter 13.

In one instance, our youngest, Karissa, registered for twelve college credit hours (mostly math and science courses for pre-med majors, I should add). At the same time, the neighborhood school required her to take an additional three classes on the high school campus. This was clearly an unreasonable demand. Twelve credit hours are considered a full course load at most four-year institutions, and there was no rationale for requiring her to take extra high school classes.

We also felt that the neighborhood school somewhat discouraged interest in dual enrollment. The guidance counselor regularly complained about the extra work it caused her. At the same time, the district heavily promoted its AP and IB programs while remaining almost silent about dual enrollment.

Eventually, the local community college convinced us to transfer to what Colorado calls an early college, a decision we've never regretted. The early college functioned like a traditional high school while also focusing on equipping students for collegiate studies. This allowed them to earn as many free college credits as possible. Once students fulfilled their high school requirements, they were free to concentrate solely on college coursework. This aligned more with our family's goal of maximizing the number of free college credits our kids could earn.

Through that experience, we came to realize that many states offer a variety of pathways for earning college credit during high school. Exploring these options and gathering the right information is essential. It's the best way to find the path that fits your family's goals and build an effective plan for your child's education.

To Recap:

1. Review school and district websites to learn about available dual enrollment options in your area.
2. Contact your neighborhood school's guidance counselors and district representatives and ask them to provide as much information as possible about the dual enrollment program. Let them know you want to make the most of this opportunity.
3. Check your state's department of education website; state guidelines may reveal benefits your district hasn't shared.
4. Most importantly, reach out to your local community college for information about dual enrollment opportunities in your area. They want your business and often have tips and tricks that aren't readily available.
5. Find out if there are any early colleges in your area. These schools typically function like a traditional high school but focus on preparing students for college-level work, helping them maximize the number of credits they can earn.
6. Don't be afraid to pivot. If your current dual enrollment situation isn't working or you're facing constant resistance, consider transferring to a different opportunity that better suits your family's needs.

Above all, don't assume that the information provided by a guidance counselor, district representative, website, or any other authority is fully accurate or complete. Keep researching and asking questions until you have the answers you need. After all, your tax dollars are funding your child's education, and you have every right to make the most of them.

CHAPTER 4:
GETTING EVERYONE ON BOARD WITH DUAL ENROLLMENT

My kids didn't have a choice regarding taking college classes while in high school. Long before they entered high school, my husband and I informed them that they could expect to participate in a dual enrollment program. We wanted them to experience what college-level work was like while it was still free. If they enjoyed it, great—they'd earn credit and gain confidence. If they didn't, we would know early on without having spent any money on tuition.

While they were nervous about the coursework and somewhat concerned about doing something not many of their friends were doing, we believed that the benefits outweighed the challenges. To alleviate their apprehension, we promised to support them in any way we could and provide any resources they needed to be successful. We also allowed them to select the dual enrollment program they felt most comfortable with based on the various options available in our area. In the end, while they were initially apprehensive, both of my daughters ended up really enjoying their dual enrollment classes and even preferred them over traditional high school courses.

Regardless, I understand that getting your family on board with the idea of taking college classes while in high school might be a challenge. However, I believe that if you approach it thoughtfully and explain the benefits, they will eventually embrace the idea. Allow me to share a few strategies to help you make your case.

Focus on the Financial Benefits

Do a cost comparison to see how much money you can save by using dual enrollment compared to traditional college expenses. Most of these programs are either free or very low cost, so your family could potentially save thousands of dollars. At the same time, caution them about the dangers of student loan debt. In my blog post *Stories of Devastating Debt After Sending Kids to College* on FinishCollegeinHighSchool.com, I share stories of the catastrophic debt families incur after sending their kids to college. To date, there are also 171 pages of additional stories on StudentDebtCrisis.org. While some people can manage their student loans, hundreds of thousands of Americans have had their lives completely destroyed by them. In his book *The Student Loan Scam*, Alan Collinge of Student Loan Justice makes a compelling argument that the entire student loan industry is corrupt, predatory, and highly unethical.[5] Given this, along with other reasons I'll discuss in Chapter 16, I believe student loans should be avoided in most situations.

Highlight the Academic Benefits

Explain how dual enrollment allows students to get a head

start on their college education, helping them graduate earlier. Emphasize that college-level courses are typically taught by professors with master's degrees or PhDs, who are also often experienced professionals. This can offer a more rigorous and rewarding academic experience compared to traditional high school classes.[6]

Share How Dual Enrollment Helps Students Prepare for College Life

Taking college classes while in high school will immerse students in a more independent, self-motivated learning environment, which can make the transition to college smoother. Both of my daughters thrived their first year after transferring to a four-year university. While many college students struggle with managing time, workload, reading a syllabus, college-level writing, and a variety of other challenges, my kids had been practicing these skills for three years during high school, making the transition much easier for them. Dual enrollment also allows students to explore different subjects, helping clarify their field of study and career path. Additionally, it's a great way for students to determine if they even want to go to college. As I mentioned earlier, many students decide against college after taking just a few college classes.

Share That Dual Enrollment Will Strengthen Their Resume

The ability to list college-level courses on their transcripts can help your kids stand out to future colleges, scholarship committees, and employers. It demonstrates that they're committed to their education and ready to take on challenges. When colleges see dual enrollment classes on a transcript, they won't have to question a student's ability to succeed; they'll have clear proof the student can handle college-level work.

Additionally, as a result of dual enrollment, my kids were able to add an associate degree to their job applications by 18, and they never had trouble finding jobs while in college. Employers often hired them on the spot during their initial interviews. During her first year at the university, Caitlyn even secured a job on campus as the manager of the college radio station. They trusted her to completely rebuild the station after it had been silent for two years due to COVID.

Address Common Concerns

Financial Concerns: In many situations, dual enrollment is free or very low-cost since the state covers tuition for high school students. If there are additional expenses, such as books and college fees, they usually pale in comparison to what you would pay at a four-year university.

Social Life: If they're concerned about missing out on typical high school experiences, explain that dual enrollment students can still participate in high school activities, clubs, and sports while taking college classes. Additionally, they may have even more time for social activities since they won't be at the high school for six to seven hours each day. My daughters preferred dual enrollment for this reason.

Workload: If your family is concerned about the additional workload, reassure them that while it can be challenging, you're committed to helping your student balance it with their high school responsibilities. Let them know they can start slowly by taking just one or two classes and gradually add more as their confidence grows. Also, assure them that support will be available for time management and academic help whenever it's needed. (You can find specifics on how to help in Chapters 7 and 12.)

To make this more tangible, see my youngest daughter's junior-year schedule at the end of this chapter. It shows how she balanced dual enrollment with high school classes, activities, and social life at our neighborhood school.

Share Success Stories

If you know other students who have successfully taken college classes while in high school, share their stories or arrange for your child to meet with their families. Sometimes, hearing about someone else's positive experience can help ease concerns. I also share success stories on FinishCollegeinHighSchool.com and on Instagram at @ShelleyBranine. Additionally, you can share statistics, as research shows that students who take college classes in high school tend to perform better at four-year universities.

Meet with a Counselor or College Rep

If possible, invite your family to meet with a school counselor or a representative from the college offering dual enrollment. A conversation with a professional might reassure them about the program's legitimacy and the support they will receive.

Ultimately, once your family gains a better understanding of dual enrollment, I believe the benefits will far outweigh the challenges, and they will naturally support the decision. Helping them see the financial savings, academic advantages, and the ability to explore career paths early on will highlight the long-term value of this opportunity.

To Recap:

1. Help your family understand that dual enrollment is a significant financial benefit that will allow your kids to save thousands of dollars on a college education.
2. Reassure them that they will gain a much more rigorous and rewarding academic experience that will push them to excel.
3. Let them know that dual enrollment will prepare them for college life and strengthen their resumes, opening more job opportunities both after high school and during college.
4. Address their concerns by reassuring them that you will help balance the college workload, provide necessary support, and ensure they can still enjoy a typical teenage social life.
5. Help them understand that they can and will succeed in dual enrollment. Share success stories and, if needed, meet with an academic counselor to discuss how others have thrived.

Once your family understands the benefits and sees the support available, I'm confident any doubts will begin to fade. When they recognize how dual enrollment can save money, boost their academics, and open doors for the future, they'll be on board. In the end, they'll see that taking college classes in high school is not only manageable, but a smart decision that sets students up for long-term success.

Karissa's Weekly Schedule – Junior Year, 1st Semester

Time	Monday	Tuesday	Wednesday	Thursday	Friday
8:20-9:54 Period 1	High School Algebra 2	High School U.S. History	High School Algebra 2	High School U.S. History	9:20-10:31 Period 1 (Late Start)
9:59-11:36 Period 2	College Eng 102 10:00-11:15 At comm college	High School Off Period Study Hall	College Eng 102 10:00-11:15 At comm college	High School Off Period Study Hall	10:36-11:06 Seminar Home Room
11:41-12:17 Lunch	College Pub Speak 11:30-12:45 At comm college	Lunch	College Pub Speak 11:30-12:45 At comm college	Lunch	11:11-12:22 Period 2
12:22-1:56 Period 3	Off Period Lunch Return to School	High School Off Period Study Hall	Off Period Lunch Return to School	High School Off Period Study Hall	12:27-1:03 Lunch
2:01-3:35 Period 4	High School Yearbook	High School General Science	High School Yearbook	High School General Science	1:08-3:35 Periods 3 & 4
After School	Poms Practice 4:00-6:00	Worked at Olive Garden	Dance Technique Class 8:30-9:30	Poms Practice 4:00-6:00	Football and Basketball Games
Notes	Had permission to leave early during first period to attend her college class	Was given an additional off period / study hall since she was taking college classes			No college classes on Fridays; high school schedule alternated between the Mon/Wed and Tues/Thur rotations

On weekends, Karissa divided her time between socializing, studying, and working shifts at Olive Garden.

CHAPTER 5:
HELPING YOUR STUDENT CHOOSE A
MAJOR AND CAREER PATH

Both of our daughters were able to identify a preferred major and career path after taking just a few college classes, something I don't believe would have happened as early had they only participated in traditional high school courses. While students aren't required to choose a field of study right away, dual enrollment offers opportunities to explore their interests early, and there are several steps you can take to help your kids discover their career path at their own pace.

Help Them Self-Reflect

It can be helpful to journal or make a list of ideas. Begin by reflecting on various aspects, such as how your child excels in both academic and non-academic settings, what they enjoy, and the people or experiences that have had a lasting impact on them. For instance, our youngest, Karissa, is a dancer, and she was required to attend physical therapy due to an injury she incurred during her sophomore year of high school. She developed such a strong bond with her physical therapist that she went on to write a scholarship-winning essay about her experience and also decided she wanted to become a physical therapist before she even graduated high school.

The self-reflection process may also involve asking others what they see as strengths in your child. Similarly, career centers at many colleges offer a wealth of resources to support this process, helping students explore their strengths and potential career paths. In these centers, students can receive career counseling and advising, explore internship options, and take personality and skills assessments to determine careers that might be a good fit. By using these tools and gathering relevant information, students can identify several possible career paths to consider as they plan for their future. Additional self-assessment tools are also included at the end of this chapter to further support this exploration.

Guide Them in Researching Different Career Concentrations

Based on your self-reflection, begin to research various career concentrations. Look into industries that align with your child's interests and values. It is also important to consider future trends in the fields, including job market demand, technological advancements, and economic shifts. A career can significantly affect your quality of life, so you and your kids should also evaluate lifestyle factors such as work-life balance, work hours, job location, onsite versus remote work, industry stability, stress levels, and physical demands.

While we all want our kids to work in a job they love, they

should also consider a job's salary in their decision-making process. It's crucial to choose a career path that offers financial stability. Erik and I graduated college in 1997 with degrees that led to low-paying jobs—Erik pursued radio broadcasting, and I became a teacher—and we chose to live in Colorado, a state with one of the highest costs of living. We struggled for years to make ends meet and carried $50,000 in combined student loan debt, which made it even harder to cover our living expenses. Eventually, we transitioned into higher-paying careers, but the experience taught us some hard lessons about the long-term financial impact of career and education choices.

When thinking about finances, it's essential to consider not just potential salary, but also the educational requirements of a chosen career. Will your child need a graduate degree? Can they realistically afford that additional education? Because of our own experience, we made sure our daughters were realistic when selecting their college majors, encouraging them to weigh their interests against future job prospects, salary expectations, and the cost of required education.

Once your child has narrowed down a few career possibilities, consider arranging a job-shadowing experience. If you know someone in that field, ask if they'd be willing to let a student observe them on the job. If not, you can reach out directly to organizations to see if they offer shadowing opportunities. Career fairs and community centers are also great places to connect with professionals in various industries, and local chambers of commerce or college career centers may also be able to facilitate introductions. Job shadowing can give students valuable firsthand insight and help them quickly determine whether a specific career path feels like the right fit.

Encourage Them to Take College Classes

Encourage your child to begin taking courses that align with the requirements of the fields they're considering. When choosing classes, it's essential they pick a good professor. A dull or overly demanding instructor can turn students off to a subject, while an inspiring professor can open doors to unexpected interests. In the next chapter, I'll explain how to identify a great professor.

Karissa had a pretty good idea that she wanted to be a physical therapist when she started taking college classes. Then she took anatomy with her favorite teacher of all time, a tatted-up doctor and beloved instructor at the college. By the end of the class, she was confident that she wanted to be a physical therapist and was excited to continue learning more about the human body.

Most of the students I've worked with have been able to determine a major and career field after taking just a few college classes. Some have even quickly concluded that college is not for them and were able to narrow down their career choices to roles that do not require a college degree. The best thing about dual enrollment is that students are not paying for the classes or acquiring student loan debt, so they are free to explore many options at no cost.

It's important to note that once your child decides on a

career path, it's perfectly fine for them to change their mind. We actually encouraged our oldest, Caitlyn, to reconsider her major. Since elementary school, when she was always the top seller of Girl Scout cookies, she dreamed of studying business marketing. However, Caitlyn has a seizure disorder that has historically impacted her memory. She's even had seizures that caused her to lose an entire semester of learning, particularly in subjects like math and science, which rely on the left side of the brain. While researching marketing programs, we discovered that most business degrees require calculus, two semesters of accounting, and statistics. Knowing Caitlyn's challenges with math, we encouraged her to pursue a communications and marketing degree, which had a lighter math load. As a result, she graduated with an above-average GPA and experienced much less stress.

On the other hand, it shouldn't take years for young people to determine what they want to do. Students who continually change their minds or lack a sense of direction run the risk of increased financial burden, lack of motivation, frustration, stress, anxiety, and fear of making the wrong choice.

When working with young adults struggling to choose a college major or career path, I encourage them to reengage in self-reflection and revisit exploring different career options. If they still struggle to come up with a plan, I suggest that while in high school, they take as many general education classes as possible or learn a trade. This will allow them to take a year or two off after high school to gain life experience, which often helps them decide on a career path. Then, if they choose to continue with college, they will already have a year or two completed and paid for. Another option is for them to select a more general major that can lead to a variety of careers, such as business, marketing, or communications. Ultimately, the goal is to give them the experiences and resources they need to make an informed decision.

Guidance in career planning is especially important at this stage of development. Young people often need help choosing a career path because the part of the brain responsible for decision-making, planning, and impulse control (the prefrontal cortex) does not fully mature until the mid-twenties. This developmental lag explains why they benefit from the presence of mature adults when making critical life choices, especially those that will affect the rest of their lives. Students are being asked to make big decisions in their late teens and early twenties, and they need a loving adult to walk with them through the process.

To Recap:

1. Stay actively engaged as your child explores college majors and potential career paths.
2. Help them reflect on their academic and non-academic interests, as well as experiences that have shaped them.
3. Research different career concentrations, considering factors like job location, work hours, work-life balance, and salary.
4. Encourage your child to take college courses that help them explore potential career paths. A good professor can help students determine whether they enjoy the content and excel in it.

5. It's normal for students to reconsider their major and career path, but the decision-making process shouldn't drag on for years. If they're struggling to decide, gaining real-world experience can provide valuable clarity.

Deciding on a career path can feel overwhelming for young adults, but with the right guidance, they can gradually gain direction and confidence. Taking college classes in high school is one of the most effective ways for students to explore their interests and potential career paths. It allows them to sample different subject areas and discover what excites them, without the financial pressure. In our family's experience, just a few college courses helped both of our daughters clarify their goals and confidently choose their career paths before graduating high school.

On the other hand, they also had a friend who dropped out of college just one class short of earning an associate degree. He realized he didn't enjoy school and decided instead to pursue work as a carpenter at a cabinet-making company—a decision he's never regretted. Fortunately, because he participated in a dual enrollment program, he never accumulated any student loan debt. While still in high school, he took college classes and ultimately determined that college wasn't the right path for him. Even better, the state of Colorado covered his tuition while he explored his options.

If only all eighteen-year-olds had that kind of opportunity.

Resources

Government resources

- U.S. Bureau of Labor Statistics (BLS): Provides occupational outlooks, industry profiles, and detailed information on job responsibilities, education requirements, and salary data.
- CareerOneStop: A service of the U.S. Department of Labor, offering career exploration tools, job search resources, and local training opportunities

Assessment tools

- MyNextMove: Provides an interest assessment based on the Holland Code (RIASEC) theory to match your interests with potential careers.
- CareerExplorer: Offers a comprehensive career test based on the Holland Code and Myers-Briggs Type Indicator (MBTI) to identify suitable career paths.
- CareerOneStop: Offers various tools and resources, including skills assessment, career exploration, and salary information.

CHAPTER 6:
HELPING YOUR STUDENT CHOOSE THEIR FIRST COLLEGE CLASSES

As a parent, it can be scary to imagine your teenager taking college classes. We wonder: Will my kids be safe on a college campus? What if they miss out on the high school experience? Can they really handle college-level coursework? Should they be taking AP or IB classes instead? Is it wise to pursue something so different from what our friends are doing? I address many of these concerns at FinishCollegeinHighSchool.com, where I also share my belief that any high school student can succeed in college-level classes or technical school, provided they have the support and resources they need—and this begins with helping them choose the best classes.

When choosing their first classes, I recommend students select subjects they find highly interesting or areas in which they already excel. Our youngest, Karissa, really wanted to learn sign language, and even though we knew the class wouldn't transfer to a four-year university, we encouraged her to enroll because we were sure she would enjoy the content. My kids also started with college English because, if needed, I knew I could support them with the course if they struggled. The bottom line: Start where you know your family will be successful.

Next, and this is huge, refer to websites where students can rate and review college professors. Our family loved RateMyProfessors.com. When choosing classes, always utilize sites like this or recommendations from other students. I sincerely believe that, as long as your kids work hard and fulfill the requirements, a good professor will almost always ensure their success in the course. With a less favorable professor, their success becomes uncertain. On RateMyProfessors.com, instructors are rated based on both the quality and difficulty of their courses. You can also read comments from other students about their experiences with the professor.

You should also make sure your student registers early, as the best professors' classes fill up quickly. Colleges often release the upcoming semester's schedule before the registration windows open, so we always created a few scenarios in advance. Then, when it came time to register, we were able to quickly select classes on the earliest day possible. This is especially important as your child gets closer to graduation and has fewer options for courses to complete.

When it is time to select classes:

- Make a list of all the classes your child wants or needs to take. Keep in mind that they may need to meet with a high school guidance counselor or community college advisor first.
- Consider the days and times that the classes are offered to make sure they will fit into your child's schedule.

- Take note of the difficulty of the courses and make sure to balance challenging classes with content that comes easily or is more enjoyable. There is nothing worse than taking a full load of classes that are extremely difficult or unappealing.
- Always refer to a website that provides professor reviews or seek the insight of other students. Some professors make their classes unnecessarily difficult and/or grade too harshly. In a few instances, we had our daughters take a class at a different community college and then transfer the credits back to their local school because the professor had a better reputation.

Finally, if possible, once your child has selected their classes, wait a few days before registering so you have time to think it over. Sometimes, we came up with better ideas when we gave ourselves a few days to reflect. Of course, most colleges will allow students to change their schedules if needed, so don't feel like anything is set in stone. You can always adjust at the beginning of the semester if you find a better opportunity or discover that a particular class isn't a good fit.

One semester, Karissa completed early registration and chose Anatomy 1 for pre-med students in an accelerated eight-week format. Normally, I would have been concerned about her taking such a difficult class in such a short amount of time, but the professor had outstanding ratings, so I was fairly confident she would be successful. She could have also registered for accelerated Anatomy 2, but I felt it would be too much and encouraged her to complete her history requirement instead. We chose a professor with good reviews, but when she arrived on the first day of class, she discovered that the history professor had been replaced by someone new and unengaging. She was concerned that the class would be unnecessarily difficult, so she decided to drop History and take accelerated Anatomy 2 instead. It ended up being a wise decision. She earned high grades in both Anatomy classes, and to this day, they are her favorite classes of all time. She even cried when she had to say goodbye to the professor. At graduation, she ran up and gave him a big hug, and we were able to express the significant impact he had on her life.

In another instance, Caitlyn was trying to decide between two classes. One professor was new and didn't have any reviews on RateMyProfessors.com, and the other had only two reviews. Because we didn't have a lot of information, she registered for both classes and attended the first day of each to determine which professor seemed like a better fit for her. Then, she immediately dropped the less appealing class to avoid being charged for it. Meeting the professor and reviewing the syllabus helped her decide which class she preferred.

The classes your kids choose will play an integral role in their success with college coursework. Our kids graduated with strong GPAs, and this is largely due to the classes they selected. Yes, they worked hard, but we also created a schedule that ensured success before they even began each semester.

As your kids progress in dual enrollment, their confidence in handling college-level courses will grow. At that point, it's wise to start looking ahead and ensuring that the classes they choose align with their long-term goals, especially if they plan to attend a four-year university. While transferring credits to another college is usually straightforward, there can still be confusion about which credits will carry over. That's why this common concern deserves a closer look.

Keep in mind that some dual enrollment programs require parents to reimburse the school if a student earns below a C in a class. A low grade could also affect your child's GPA and limit future scholarship opportunities. My goal is to help you save as much money as possible, and the best way to do that is by helping your student choose the right classes—and succeed in them. With thoughtful planning and the right support, your kids can not only survive college classes in high school, they can truly thrive.

To Recap:

1. Start with classes your child finds interesting or excels in.
2. Register early; the best classes fill up fast!
3. Make a list of required or desired classes, including available days and times.
4. Balance challenging courses with content that comes easily or is more enjoyable.
5. Choose favorable instructors using professor review sites or peer recommendations.

Myth:
Universities Don't Accept Community College Credits

A common misconception is that dual enrollment credits won't transfer to a four-year university. Some families even hear this from guidance counselors, which can make the myth sound more believable.

The truth:
- Most in-state and many private universities accept dual enrollment credits.
- The majority of U.S. states have rules that ensure core college classes and associate degrees transfer to public universities.
- Remedial or highly specialized courses may not transfer—but they often still count as electives.
- Elite schools like Harvard and Yale are exceptions, but they also restrict AP and IB credit.

Bottom line: Dual enrollment credits usually transfer and can save families thousands in tuition. Don't let this myth keep you from taking advantage of a smart opportunity.

For more on this topic see my accompanying blog post "Myth: Universities Don't Accept Community College Credits" on FinishCollegeinHighSchool.com.

6. If possible, wait a few days before registering to reflect and ensure you make the right choices.
7. Don't be afraid to pivot. If your child starts a class and it doesn't feel like the right fit, consider switching early to avoid fees or falling behind.
8. Once your child is confident with college courses, make sure to choose classes that align with their long-term goals and will transfer to a four-year institution.

Registering for classes is one of the most important things your student will do. They're not just creating a schedule, they're building momentum for everything that comes next. High school students can succeed in college-level courses. As parents, our job is to help them plan wisely, manage their workload, and provide the support they need to reach their goals.

CHAPTER 7:
SETTING YOUR STUDENT UP FOR SUCCESS IN DUAL ENROLLMENT

I understand that college isn't the right fit for everyone. However, I also believe that with commitment, any student can succeed—and that includes those still in high school. It's also important to remember that most dual enrollment students will need some degree of support, and some will require more help than others.

We approached our kids' dual enrollment experience as a family; everyone contributed and helped as needed, and we, as parents, stayed actively involved in their education from their first college class through graduation. Students often need significant support in their initial dual enrollment courses, but as they adapt to the rhythm and expectations of college work, the level of assistance can gradually be reduced. This chapter will provide valuable information to help you stay involved and ensure your student's success.

The syllabus rules all.

I highly recommend printing the course syllabus at the start of any college class and reviewing it in depth with your child. College professors are very different from high school teachers; they don't provide handholding or reminders, and they only offer assistance when a student requests it. This can be a significant adjustment for high schoolers. Because of this, I regularly reviewed the syllabus with my kids until I was confident they could manage it independently.

I often told my girls that college professors aren't particularly concerned if you fail, so it's up to you to take ownership of your assignments, pay close attention to instructions and grading rubrics, and keep track of deadlines and due dates. Because of a seizure disorder, our eldest, Caitlyn, struggles with her memory and has difficulty managing large amounts of information and specific details. It really helped her to print each syllabus and highlight assignments as she completed and submitted them. At the beginning of each term, she also mapped out the due dates for every assignment she needed to complete throughout the semester and referred to her academic planner daily.

One of the most important things you can do is emphasize the importance of carefully following the course syllabus. During the final semester of her associate degree, Caitlyn misread her accounting syllabus and failed to turn in 15 assignments. The syllabus listed "recommended" due dates for the assignments, and Caitlyn initially interpreted this to mean the assignments were optional. However, the professor intended for all assignments to be submitted by the end of the semester and simply encouraged students to follow the "recommended" due dates to stay on track. Caitlyn didn't realize she was missing 15 assignments until she received her final grade—a D.

Our dual enrollment program required parents to pay for any classes in which a student earned below a C, so we always told our kids that they would need to cover the cost if they did not pass. As a result, Caitlyn appealed to the professor. She apologized and explained her misunderstanding, sharing that she has processing issues due to her seizure disorder and doesn't always understand instructions clearly. (This is true, I'll add. We wouldn't have allowed her to lie or make excuses.)

Since we were always careful to select the best instructors, Caitlyn caught a break. Her kind and gracious professor gave her two extra days to submit as many of the missing assignments as possible. So, she worked on accounting around the clock for 48 hours and managed to raise her grade to a B. To this day, whenever Caitlyn signs a high school graduation card for a friend, she writes eight words before signing her name: "Always read the syllabus and follow it carefully."

Warning: Many students are not ready for college-level writing.

While our daughters were successful in middle-school and high-school English, neither was fully prepared for college-level writing. Unfortunately, this is the case for many young adults. Instead of preparing students for college-level writing, most high schools focus on writing for standardized tests. In addition to a strong grasp of grammar, punctuation, and sentence structure, college students must also be able to think critically, conduct academic research, and cite sources in various citation styles.

The best professors understand this and typically spend the entire English 101 course (or its equivalent) teaching students how to write at a collegiate level. While my daughters' college English professors did a great job, I still felt the need to support them in their initial writing-intensive classes, including history and social sciences. The bonus chapter at the end of this book, "Writing with Confidence at the College Level," provides insight on how you can help your child master the writing skills required in college. However, if writing isn't your area of strength, you might consider hiring a tutor (more information on finding tutors is in Chapter 12), or your child can also get free help through the college's writing center. Keep in mind that professors will not reach out to you if your child is struggling with writing or any other content area. This is why I recommend checking in regularly with your kids to ensure they are successfully meeting the writing requirements for all their classes.

<u>You are the parent. You should have access to grades.</u>

To avoid surprises like our accounting nightmare, it's important to regularly ask your kids to show you their grades. In that particular situation, it wouldn't have helped because the professor didn't update grades until the last day of class. However, in most cases, you should be able to monitor your student's class performance regularly.

At many schools, your kids can notify the college in writing that parents are allowed to access their grades. Keep in mind that under the Family Educational Rights and Privacy Act (FERPA), if a student does not grant permission, the college cannot release any student information to parents, even if the student is a minor.

While we wanted our daughters to maintain strong grades to help earn scholarships, we were also mindful of the dual enrollment policy and didn't want to be forced to pay for a class due to a low grade. As a result, we did our best to keep a close eye on their grades.

<u>Set boundaries around the support you will provide for your kids.</u>

In the beginning, Caitlyn had a habit of asking for help the night before a big project or paper was due. This became extremely stressful and frustrating for Erik and me. As a result, we had to set clear guidelines for how and when we would help her. Erik required at least 24 hours' notice if she needed help, and I asked for a week's notice, since I was traveling regularly for work. This gave us the time we needed to plan, prepare, and take care of our personal commitments before carving out time to help her.

I also encouraged my kids to complete as much of the assignment as possible on their own before asking for help. That way, I didn't have to devote as much time, since they were handling some of the work independently.

Finally, I want to reiterate that if you don't have the time or comfort level to help your kids with their classes, they can seek support from the college through tutoring or writing centers. They'll just need to plan ahead to ensure they get the help they need on time. If they wait until the last minute, these centers may not be available.

With the right support structure in place, any high schooler can thrive in college classes. Dual enrollment not only accelerates their academic progress but also helps them develop critical life skills like independence, responsibility, and time management. By staying actively involved in their academic journey, you are helping prepare your kids for success in college and also in the real world.

To Recap:

1. Understand that your child will likely need some degree of support. Most students require a lot of help initially but become more independent as they learn the rhythm and expectations of college coursework.
2. Review the syllabus with your student at the beginning of each semester and periodically throughout the course until they can manage the class requirements independently.
3. Support your student if they are not yet ready for college-level writing. Monitor their progress in English and other writing-intensive courses, and ensure they have the resources they need to succeed.
4. Frequently check your child's grades to ensure they are passing all their classes and staying on top of their coursework.
5. Set boundaries on how and when you will support your child.

While dual enrollment is a commitment and a serious undertaking, it is not unlike other educational opportunities. In truth, parents should remain heavily involved in their kids' education from early childhood through graduation.

Supporting our daughters while they completed two years of college in high school wasn't easy, but it was worth it. Dual enrollment saved us $60,000–$80,000 or more, and we believe that the hard work was worth every penny.

CHAPTER 8:
COLLEGE AND FINANCIAL PLANNING: ADVICE FOR DUAL ENROLLMENT STUDENTS AFTER HIGH SCHOOL GRADUATION

Congratulations! You've discovered one of the best-kept secrets. Your family has saved thousands of dollars through dual enrollment. Now is not the time to start racking up student loan debt. This chapter will discuss ways to pay for college after taking advantage of dual enrollment during high school, beginning with an important question:

Does your child truly want—or need—a four-year degree?

Through dual enrollment, many students discover that they don't want to continue with college at all. Others find that taking just a few classes helps them easily identify a college major and career path. Either way, dual enrollment often provides clarity early on, before students commit years of time and thousands of dollars toward a degree they may not need.

Rethinking College with Mike Rowe

Author and TV host Mike Rowe has been one of the most outspoken voices challenging the idea that every young person must earn a four-year degree. He reminds us that there are many valuable, well-paying paths outside of the traditional college track.

"America is lending money it doesn't have to kids who can't pay it back to train them for jobs that no longer exist. That's nuts." Mike Rowe, creator of *Dirty Jobs*.

Mike Rowe's message is simple:

- College isn't the only path—and it shouldn't always be the default.
- Cost matters—students must weigh return on investment, not just emotion.
- All work has value—whether it requires a degree or not.

Rowe's perspective echoes what I hear from many dual enrollment students: as soon as they start taking college classes, they begin to clarify their interests, narrow their choices, and often identify a career path as early as eleventh or twelfth grade. Sometimes they even discover that college isn't the right path for them at all. And what a great realization to have before paying full tuition.

For more on this topic, see my accompanying blog post "Myth: Everyone Needs to Go to College on FinishCollegeinHighSchool.com.

<u>Take advantage of additional opportunities to earn free or discounted college credits</u>. Below are several options that can help reduce the cost of education.

- CLEP (College Level Examination Program) exams let students earn college credit by proving subject knowledge in areas such as history, math, or foreign languages without taking the course. Exams cost less than $100 and are accepted for credit by over 2,900 colleges and universities nationwide. Passing can save students both time and thousands of dollars in tuition.
- Modern States Education Alliance is a nonprofit that provides free online prep courses for CLEP exams. When students complete a course, they can receive a voucher that covers the exam fee and sometimes even the test center fee, making it possible to earn credits at no cost.
- TEL Learning offers self-paced online courses in partnership with several four-year universities. The courses range from $75 to $225, which is considerably less than the cost at a university.
- In most cases, students can complete all general education requirements at a community college, online or during the summer while attending a four-year university. This is a cost-effective option since community college courses are typically more affordable. Both of my kids completed their general studies this way, either during high school or over the summer while finishing their university degrees.
- Most universities allow students to transfer up to half of the credits needed for their degree—usually

around 60 of the 120 required. Some schools may accept up to 90 credits or more. It's important for students to stay within these limits, as taking unnecessary courses at community colleges can waste both time and money, even though those courses are more affordable.

- Colorado offers the TREP (Teacher Recruitment Education and Preparation) program, which allows high school students who plan to become teachers to earn two years of free college after graduation. TREP is available at most Colorado community colleges and some four-year universities and is designed to support students pursuing a career in education.

- Florida Bright Futures Scholarship is a merit-based program that provides tuition assistance to eligible Florida high school graduates. It covers 100% of tuition and fees for Florida Academic Scholars (FAS) and 75% for Florida Medallion Scholars (FMS) at public colleges and universities in Florida. The award applies for up to 120 credit hours toward a bachelor's degree.

- Nevada's Millennium Scholarship provides up to $10,000 in tuition for eligible Nevada high school graduates attending in-state colleges or universities. To qualify, students must be state residents and meet specific GPA, ACT/SAT, and high school coursework requirements.

- Tennessee Promise is a last-dollar scholarship, meaning it covers the remaining tuition and fees not covered by the Pell Grant, the Tennessee HOPE Scholarship, or the Tennessee Student Assistance

Award. It will pay for up to two years of college at any Tennessee community college or technical school.

Above all, students should choose a college they can afford.

Unfortunately, many are encouraged to simply "follow their dreams" without considering the long-term financial impact. Young adults often fall into the trap of believing they must attend their "dream college," making decisions based on emotions rather than financial reality. This mindset can lead to massive debt and regret.

I recommend that students focus on two or three key factors they value most in a college, such as location, clubs, sports, student life, or academic programs. Then they should choose an affordable school that best meets their needs.

Websites like Student Loan Justice and The Student Debt Crisis feature hundreds of heartbreaking testimonies from people who chased their "dream school" only to find themselves buried in debt, sometimes without even completing their degree. These stories underscore how important it is for families to weigh cost just as heavily as personal preference when making college decisions. You can find more information on the concept of the "dream college" in Chapter 16.

Students should apply for scholarships, grants, work-study, and tuition reimbursement opportunities.

However, it's important to note that scholarships are not

as easy to obtain as many might think. In fact, they are usually highly competitive and have specific eligibility requirements; more detailed information on scholarships will be provided in Chapter 15. Grants, on the other hand, are more readily available, but because they are federally funded, they are only offered to families whose combined income falls below a certain threshold. Work-study positions are also need-based and even more limited than grants, so not all eligible students will receive them.

In addition to these options, students can also explore opportunities with companies that offer tuition reimbursement. Employers such as Starbucks, Chipotle, and The Home Depot provide assistance for employees pursuing their bachelor's degrees and can help reduce the financial burden of college.

Another powerful option is the U.S. military, which offers some of the best tuition benefits available. Programs like ROTC often cover all tuition and fees, with some also providing a housing stipend. In return, students must commit to serving in the military for a certain number of years after receiving the scholarship. Additionally, all branches of the military offer 100% tuition assistance for students who enlist in the reserves or active duty.

Create a plan for how your family will pay for college.

We were able to save some money for our daughters' college, but it wasn't nearly enough for a four-year university. We were adamant that they would not take out any student loans, so they had to consider the price tag before selecting a college. Our oldest, Caitlyn, ran out of college funds during her final year of school. She had enough money for tuition but could not afford to live on campus. We gave her two choices: she could either live at home and take online classes, or work over the summer to save money for on-campus housing. She chose to work two jobs and was able to pay her housing bill when she returned to school in the fall.

Help your kids understand that college is a significant expense.

Many students don't realize this until after they graduate or drop out, and their student loans start coming due. One of my friends developed a brilliant plan to help her kids grasp this reality. They finished high school with two years of college credits, chose an affordable university, and received partial scholarships. Since student loans were not an option, my friend paid her kids' tuition bills at the beginning of each semester and required them to pay her back throughout the term. If tuition was $4,000, they made five monthly payments of $800. After they passed all their classes, she returned the money to cover the next semester's tuition, but had they not passed, she would have required them to cover the costs of retaking any failed courses themselves.

This approach not only helped her kids understand the expense of education but also held them accountable for their grades. The kids lived at home to save money, but one really wanted to live on campus. So, she got a job as a resident assistant and received free room and board. As a result, these kids graduated college completely debt-free, recognize the value of their degrees, and have begun to understand the importance of financial planning.

<u>Be creative.</u>

Another friend worked concessions at professional sporting events, and all the money she earned throughout the year went into a college savings account. She enjoyed supporting the local teams while gradually saving for her son's semester college payments. Similarly, another option is to encourage your child to take one or two classes at a time and pay for them as they go. This approach helps avoid the burden of large student loans and keeps education more manageable and affordable.

<u>Student loans should almost always be avoided and only considered as a last resort in the most extreme cases.</u>

Another friend had a daughter who wanted to study engineering. After researching the potential salary of entry-level engineers and the cost of living in the area where her daughter might live, my friend felt confident that her daughter could manage student loan payments after graduation. They took out as few loans as possible, keeping in mind that colleges often encourage students to borrow the maximum amount, but students can (and should) refuse any loan money they don't need. Upon graduation, her daughter secured a high-paying job. Together, they created a loan repayment plan, and she was able to pay off her debt in just a couple of years.

Like my friend's daughter, students should carefully consider the starting salary for their chosen career and the cost of living in the area where they plan to live after college. Many young adults will struggle to afford student loan payments on top of their living expenses, and in such cases, student loans should be avoided at all costs.

It's crucial for families to understand that student loans carry significant risks. Unlike other types of loans, student loans lack consumer protections, which can quickly lead young adults into overwhelming debt and dire financial situations. For this reason, I strongly advise against taking out student loans in almost any situation. In fact, I did not allow my own kids to borrow for college; we prioritized affordable options from the beginning to protect their financial futures. You can find more information on the dangers of student loans in Chapter 16.

Most importantly, don't assume student loans are the only way to pay for college. Take the time to create a thoughtful plan, explore all options, and get creative in making college affordable. It's possible for your child to graduate debt-free by finding smarter ways to finance their education—without relying on loans.

To Recap:

1. If your student wants to attend a four-year college, help them understand the importance of choosing a school your family can afford.
2. Take advantage of additional opportunities to earn free or discounted college credits.

3. Apply for scholarships, grants, work-study, and tuition reimbursement opportunities.
4. Create a plan for how your family will pay for college and help your child understand that college is a significant expense.
5. Find creative ways to fund their education.
6. Student loans should only be considered as a last resort, and in almost all cases, they should be avoided completely.

There are many unconventional ways to pay for college, and it's important to stay positive. Young adults often accumulate massive student loan debt because they feel helpless and desperate. Instead of taking that route, we need to think outside the box. Embracing creativity and keeping an open mind can unlock possibilities you may never have imagined.

CHAPTER 9:
CAN A STUDENT WITH SPECIAL NEEDS BE SUCCESSFUL IN DUAL ENROLLMENT?

Students with special needs can not only succeed in dual enrollment programs, but with the right support systems, they can truly thrive. I've mentioned Caitlyn's struggles and the repercussions of her seizure disorder. Memory loss, processing difficulties, and challenges with multitasking, time management, and organization make academics incredibly challenging for her. Additionally, seizures have damaged the left side of her brain, affecting her ability to excel in logical subjects like math and science. Yet, despite needing significant support, she successfully completed college courses.

In high school, she was placed on a 504 plan, which the early college used to document the necessary accommodations. In addition, she worked with the disability services department at the community college to create a personalized plan focused on academic success. Due to laws protecting students with special needs, all schools, including postsecondary institutions, are required to provide the necessary services and accommodations to help them succeed.

Colleges typically don't use the same terminology for disability plans as high schools, but they still provide support for students with special needs. High schools use terms like Individualized Education Program (IEP) and 504 Plan. While colleges don't use these specific terms, they do have similar structures in place to support students with special needs. Below are explanations of these plans as used in high schools:

- An IEP is a plan used by K–12 schools for students who need special education. It outlines specific educational goals, related services, and accommodations to support the student's learning and participation in the school environment. It is developed through extensive testing and a collaborative process involving parents, educators, specialists, and school administrators. While colleges do not use IEPs, they still support students with special needs through their disability services departments.

- A 504 Plan, established under Section 504 of the Rehabilitation Act of 1973, is an educational support plan designed to provide accommodations and services to individuals with disabilities. It outlines specific provisions tailored to meet a student's needs, such as extended time on tests, preferential seating, and access to assistive technology. Obtaining a 504 Plan is less involved than qualifying for an IEP; it typically requires documentation of a medical diagnosis and a meeting with the family and school officials to develop a plan with accommodations.

Our experiences with the community college and university were even less formal than those in high school. The college's disability services department simply asked for documentation of the disability, and we provided a letter from the doctor along with the high school 504 Plan. They then helped us determine appropriate accommodations. In our experience, the colleges were extremely cooperative. They went above and beyond to find solutions that would help Caitlyn, and every time she had a seizure, they met with us to make any necessary adjustments to her plan. Due to bureaucracy and red tape, the high schools tended to be more resistant. Of course, they provided accommodations and followed the law, but they were often less generous with their support. In contrast, the colleges always seemed happy to help and were willing to do anything within their power to ensure Caitlyn's success.

Apart from working with the schools to find solutions, there were also a few things we did as a family to support Caitlyn. First, we attended every meeting that involved creating and documenting accommodations. In high school, a parent is required to attend 504 and IEP meetings, but this is not the case in college. In fact, college officials always needed to obtain Caitlyn's permission for us to attend meetings with her. Due to the Family Educational Rights and Privacy Act (FERPA), colleges will not share information with parents unless the student authorizes it. This rule applies even if the student is a minor. Therefore, parents should remain actively involved in their child's education to stay informed about what is happening at the college. Attending all meetings about your child's disability will enable you to offer valuable insights and advocate effectively when needed.

At the beginning of each semester, we also helped Caitlyn map out all her assignments for each class. We printed the syllabus and had her note the assignment due dates on two different calendars, using various colors to distinguish between classes. She used an academic planner and kept a large calendar in her room as a visual reference that she could review daily. She also added a reminder to both calendars a week before an assignment was due to give her a heads-up and prompt her to start preparing. In addition, she highlighted assignments on the syllabi as she completed and turned them in. This helped her triple-check that everything was complete. Because of her struggles with memory loss and organization, these strategies were essential in helping Caitlyn manage her assignments effectively throughout the semester, ensuring she stayed on top of her coursework.

We also checked in with Caitlyn regularly, reviewing her grades and helping her plan for upcoming assignments. At times, she needed ideas for content related to papers and presentations. On other occasions, we discovered she was struggling and encouraged her to reach out to the professor, find a tutor, or meet with disability services. Sometimes, we had to come up with a different plan to help her keep organized and stay ahead of her schoolwork. We constantly adjusted the ways we supported her based on her health, current classes, and other outside factors. It's important to remember that supporting students with special needs is not a one-size-fits-all solution; their accommodations vary based on numerous factors. Always staying apprised of the situation and seeking creative solutions tailored to your child's needs are the best things you can do to help.

Finally, don't be afraid to adjust. I've shared how we encouraged Caitlyn to switch her major from business marketing to communications and marketing. This resulted in a much lighter math load, as her biggest challenges were math and science courses. The change turned out to be a great decision, as it allowed her to play to her strengths—speaking and writing. Plus, with more free time, she was able to manage the university's radio station for three years. She got paid to do something she loved, and, at the same time, gained professional experience while developing her communication and marketing skills.

Struggling students absolutely can succeed in dual enrollment, but they need a strong support network and a willingness to advocate for themselves. There are many ways you can help, and by leveraging the right accommodations, support services, and personalized approaches, kids with special needs will be able to navigate the challenges and potentially thrive in college classes.

To Recap:

1. Collaborate with professionals at both the high school and college to develop an IEP, 504 Plan, and/or Disability Plan. These plans are essential for ensuring your child receives the accommodations and support they need.
2. Attend all planning and support meetings, including those with college disability services or academic staff, to stay informed and advocate effectively on your child's behalf.
3. At the beginning of each semester, use the syllabus to help your child map out a plan.

4. Consider using calendars, visual aids, color coding, or other organizational tools to help your child stay on track, reduce stress, and manage their schoolwork effectively.
5. Conduct regular check-ins and provide guidance as needed. Offer one-on-one support with assignments, seek out a tutor if needed, and encourage your child to reach out to the professor for help.
6. If additional support is needed, consider reaching out to the college's disability services office. They can create a new disability plan, adjust an existing one, and offer creative solutions to meet your child's needs.
7. Be open to making changes as needed. Encourage your child to seek out professors, courses, and areas of study that align with their strengths, and don't hesitate to adjust if something isn't working.

You are your child's best advocate. While college officials are typically helpful, they won't come to you if your child with special needs is struggling. Pay attention, offer support when needed, and stay proactive. There are plenty of solutions; you just have to seek them out and make sure they're put in place. With the right support, students with special needs can absolutely succeed in college.

CHAPTER 10:
CAN AN ENGLISH-LANGUAGE LEARNER BE SUCCESSFUL IN DUAL ENROLLMENT?

Colleges provide more support for English-language learners (ELLs) than ever before. Many community colleges have comprehensive English-learner programs and centers specifically designed to support any student who needs it. Funded by grants, these programs are often free of charge and include classes such as English as a Second Language, Conversational English, and Becoming a U.S. Citizen. If necessary, students can start with these programs, and once they gain confidence in the language and culture, they can decide whether to transition to standard college courses. If they choose to continue with college classes, some institutions offer orientation programs to help ELLs transition smoothly and provide additional support as needed.

For students who need further preparation, many colleges offer remedial classes. While these classes typically do not transfer to four-year universities, they are designed to prepare students for college-level coursework. Most community colleges offer remedial classes in reading, writing, math, study skills, and sometimes other subjects. These classes often feature smaller class sizes and more one-on-one attention from instructors, providing students with personalized instruction. However, it's important to note that many ELLs do not require remedial classes, as they can manage the course content effectively and independently. They may simply benefit from additional language or cultural support.

In addition to traditional academic support, many colleges offer personalized resources for ELLs, including immigrant and migrant students. These services may include guidance on degree and career planning, assistance with financial aid applications, peer mentoring, and tutoring tailored to their needs. Some institutions even offer scholarships specifically for non-native English speakers, which can provide additional financial support.

Language labs equipped with technology-based tools are another valuable resource for ELLs, helping to improve language skills through interactive learning. Additionally, some colleges facilitate language exchange programs that pair ELL students with native English speakers, promoting both language practice and cultural exchange. Writing and tutoring centers are also beneficial, providing specialized support with academic writing and English writing conventions, as well as subject-specific tutoring to promote success across different fields of study.

Finally, ELLs can reach out to their professors for additional support to ensure they receive the guidance they need to succeed. Academic advisors are also available to help with course selection, developing academic plans, and addressing any concerns regarding a student's academic progress. In some cases, accommodations such as extended exam time or language-specific resources may be provided to further support the learning experience.

Opportunities for ELL students have never been greater. With a wide range of support services available, colleges are helping them overcome language barriers and excel academically. These efforts empower students to build the confidence, skills, and knowledge needed to succeed in higher education and beyond.

To Recap:

1. Seek out programs and centers at the college that specifically support ELL students, as they offer valuable, individualized assistance and help students gain confidence.
2. If needed, begin with remedial courses. These courses help students transition into standard college-level work.
3. For academic support, take advantage of resources like language labs, writing centers, and tutoring centers.
4. Students should always reach out to their professor or academic advisor if they are struggling. Most professors are happy to help once they know a student needs support.

Most importantly, ELLs must take an active role in seeking out support and utilizing the resources available to them. While colleges offer a number of opportunities to help students improve their English skills and succeed academically, these resources won't be automatically provided. Even though ELL students participating in dual enrollment may still be in high school, they are expected to take responsibility for their learning and actively pursue the support necessary to thrive in a college setting. By doing so, they can overcome the challenges of higher education and set themselves up for success.

CHAPTER 11:
MAINTAINING A TEENAGE SOCIAL LIFE WHILE TAKING COLLEGE CLASSES

Society often paints a picture of the "perfect" teenage experience, focusing on stereotypes like friendship, dating, and fun. As a result, parents sometimes worry that their kids will miss out on the typical high school experience if they participate in dual enrollment. While these ideals can be inaccurate, they're often glorified in movies, TV shows, and social media, creating pressure for families to believe their teens need to have these experiences to be considered well-rounded or normal. I address these concerns in my blog post *Myth: My Child Will Miss Out on an Amazing High School Experience*, on FinishCollegeinHighSchool. com.

In our experience, my kids didn't miss out on anything by taking college classes in high school. They still enjoyed all the typical teenage milestones like homecoming, prom, and graduation, while also benefiting from the academic challenges of college courses. At the same time, we worked to give them a realistic view of high school and avoid any inflated expectations about their teenage years. In fact, years before my girls started high school, I received advice that helped me offer them a more grounded outlook on being a teenager.

When Caitlyn and Karissa were in middle school, a friend who is also an adolescent therapist gave me some of the best advice I've ever received. She told me to make sure my girls had multiple groups of friends from several different places. That way, when teenage drama unfolded in one of the circles, they had other friends to turn to and didn't feel isolated.

As a result, I encouraged my kids to be very intentional about making friends both inside and outside of school. Caitlyn was involved in Girl Scouts throughout high school, and all the girls in her troop attended different schools. Similarly, Karissa participated in dance, and the kids from her studio also had diverse academic experiences—some were homeschooled, others attended private or charter schools, and the rest went to various public schools.

We also encouraged our kids to stay in touch with friends from previous schools and activities. For this reason, not only did they have friends at their current schools, but they also maintained connections with kids from past schools and other activities. So, while some friendships naturally faded, they always had other circles where they could find acceptance and support.

At the same time, we encouraged them to make friends with different groups of kids at school. They connected with classmates and also got involved in afterschool clubs and activities. For example, Caitlyn participated in theater, while Karissa joined the school dance team. By building friendships both within and outside of school, they weren't concerned about lacking a social life when it came time to enroll in college classes.

Thanks to this strong network of friends, my kids were also able to easily transition to new school environments. After completing two years of high school, Caitlyn transferred to an early college, where she took college courses on a traditional high school campus with students her age. She not only maintained friendships from her previous school but also built many new relationships after transferring. The early college offered events like homecoming and prom, along with a variety of afterschool clubs and activities. Caitlyn even participated in student council, something she might not have had the chance to do at a larger high school. The early college was intentional about giving students access to the same milestone activities they would experience at a traditional high school.

In Karissa's second year of high school, she began taking dual enrollment classes while still attending her neighborhood school. Aside from making regular trips to the community college a few times a week, her social life remained largely unchanged. However, during her senior year, she made the decision to fully withdraw from the neighborhood school and attend classes exclusively at a college in downtown Denver. She had the opportunity to join the collegiate dance team and was excited for the challenge. As a result, she built strong friendships with the other young women on the team while maintaining relationships with some of the students from her former school. To this day, she considers the transfer one of the best decisions she's ever made.

Because our girls had friends in so many different circles, they were able to balance both a great social life and the challenges of college courses. The truth is that high schoolers don't have to choose between academics and socializing. By making friends both inside and outside of school, they can have the best of both worlds and enjoy the academic benefits of college while still having plenty of opportunities to hang out with friends their own age.

To Recap:

1. Don't let society's idealized view of the "perfect" teenage experience pressure your kids; help them develop realistic expectations of their high school years.
2. Encourage your kids to build friendships across different groups and settings. Diverse circles—both inside and outside of school—provide stability, confidence, and perspective when social dynamics change
3. Support involvement in a variety of activities and environments. From high school clubs and sports to volunteer opportunities and events at the community college, these experiences help teens build confidence and connection.
4. Rest assured that if your kids participate in dual enrollment at their neighborhood school, their social life will likely remain mostly unchanged.
5. Be open to exploring new educational options if your kids are ready for a change. This will allow them to maintain old friendships while meeting new people in different settings.

A fulfilling teenage social life is possible in almost any situation. The more environments your kids are exposed to, the more opportunities they'll have to meet people and build connections. Teaching them how to seek out and nurture meaningful friendships is a valuable life skill that will serve them well, both in high school and beyond.

CHAPTER 12:
WHAT TO DO IF YOUR STUDENT STRUGGLES

Both of our daughters needed support at times, and as I've mentioned, we did our best to stay involved in their education, monitor their grades and progress, and help with their assignments whenever we could. It's also important to note that we weren't afraid to seek outside help when necessary. This chapter will provide various strategies and resources to consider if your high schooler struggles in college classes.

First, it's important to understand that many young adults struggle with college classes, not just dual enrollment students. Statistics show that over 30% of U.S. college students drop out each year.[7] While I believe that our public school systems are, for the most part, doing the best they can, most are not equipped to fully prepare students for collegiate studies. They tend to focus more on graduation rates, low-performing students, and AP/IB programs than on college readiness. Additionally, high school curriculum is often more focused on standardized test preparation than on developing college-level critical thinking and problem-solving skills. Because of this, don't panic if your kids struggle. There are numerous resources and steps you can take to ensure their success.

Encourage Your Kids to Talk to the Professor

On the surface, this may seem like basic advice, but it often has a profound impact. In most cases, when students communicate that they are struggling, the professor will see that they care about the class and their grade. Keep in mind that if students don't approach the instructor, the professor may make one of two assumptions: either the student is doing fine, or they just don't care.

A friend who used to be a college professor shared with me that students rarely approached her when they were struggling. I'm not sure whether this was due to embarrassment, intimidation, or uncertainty about how to ask for help, but it's important to emphasize to your kids that they can and should contact the professor as soon as they begin to struggle. The professor will have a preferred method of contact, and students should be respectful of this and follow the appropriate steps. Our girls typically contacted the instructor via email and then set up a time to meet in person or virtually, if necessary. Professors often have office hours as well, so you should encourage your kids to take advantage of them when needed.

The good news is that most professors genuinely want to support struggling students. In fact, they often have insider knowledge and can offer unique suggestions and strategies that other students may not be aware of, such as opportunities for extra credit or one-on-one support during office hours. Many professors also remember their struggling students when submitting final grades. If a student is on the fence between two grades, and the professor knows they struggled but made a strong effort and sought help, they are often awarded the higher grade. Both of our girls experienced this pleasant surprise several times while taking college classes.

<u>Tutors Can Be Your Best Friend</u>

As I mentioned, Caitlyn has a seizure disorder that causes memory issues and learning challenges. If I worried about anyone participating in dual enrollment, it would be her. Because of her struggles, high school and college administrators developed a plan with accommodations to support her studies. We also worked closely with the college's disability services department and occasionally hired tutors when she needed extra support. The college officials and professors were really understanding and accommodating, often more compassionate and creative in finding solutions than what we experienced in high school.

On the other hand, school has always come easily to Karissa, especially when it comes to math and science. She never needed much support, except when she was taking college physics for pre-med students. As soon as she began to struggle, we connected her with a fantastic tutor called Dr. Science—which is indeed the name he goes by. In just a few sessions, he managed to get her caught up.

Again, I want to reiterate the importance of selecting quality professors, because a good instructor will reduce the need for tutors. It's also important to note that most colleges offer free tutoring centers, and some professors even have teaching assistants (TAs) whose sole purpose is to provide tutoring inside and outside of class. This was the case with Karissa's anatomy professor. The TA held additional study sessions twice a week, and the professor guaranteed that if students completed the work and attended the sessions, they would pass the class. Karissa attended all the study sessions, and not only did she earn a high grade, but she also formed great friendships with her classmates.

There are many ways to find a good tutor. Local tutors often advertise on websites such as Facebook Marketplace, Nextdoor, and Craigslist. You can also post a message detailing what you're looking for, and various tutors will typically respond. Additionally, many teachers tutor to earn extra money, and we even hired Caitlyn's favorite high school teacher to help her get through college algebra.

To save money, we also occasionally sought out college students for tutoring, as they typically charged less than professionals. The department chair at the college can often recommend good student tutors. It is most important to find a tutor as soon as your kids start to struggle. Don't wait until the end of the semester, as most tutors won't guarantee grade recovery. Yes, tutors charge for their services, but when we compared the amount spent on tutoring to the thousands of dollars saved through dual enrollment, the investment was well worth it.

Teach Your Kids How to Self-Advocate

One of the biggest mistakes people make is assuming there's no solution to the challenges they're facing and then giving up before seeking help or advocating for themselves. This was the case with one of Caitlyn's friends. She misunderstood the syllabus and fell behind in one of her classes. The not-so-helpful professor advised her to just give up and drop the class. I suggested that she appeal to the head of the department and ask for support in getting caught up. I even offered to write a "mom letter" on her behalf (moms are pretty great at writing letters like this!). Unfortunately, she assumed no one would help, and not only did she drop the class, but she also dropped out of college.

More often than not, someone will help. Your child might just need to go a few steps up the chain of command to find a solution. When I teach my kids to self-advocate, I encourage them to start with the professor. If the professor isn't helpful, they should reach out to the department chair and keep going up the authority ladder, all the way to the president if necessary. If the president isn't helpful, students can even file a formal grievance, though situations rarely ever escalate this far.

In our experience, our kids were almost always able to resolve issues directly with the professor. We only had to involve a department chair twice: once because a final grade was posted incorrectly, and again to ask for recommendations for a different professor when the current instructor wasn't a good fit for Karissa. I can't emphasize enough the importance of selecting the best professors. A good teacher truly cares and will almost always work with your kids to find a solution.

In one situation, Karissa reached out to the president of the university, but not because of an issue in a class. Her dance team was having trouble finding a safe rehearsal space. They were getting the runaround, and no one seemed interested in helping. So, Karissa contacted the president, who had her assistant set up a meeting to hear and document their concerns, as well as promise to find a suitable solution.

Teaching your kids to self-advocate is one of the best things you can do for them. I always encouraged my kids to keep the following points in mind when reaching out to a school official.

- Maintain a calm and composed tone in your message. Don't come across as angry or overly emotional.
- Start with something positive; a "thank you" or "I really enjoy your class" goes a long way.
- Don't lie, make excuses, or blame others.
- Politely share your concerns and provide specific examples of your struggles. Apologize and offer an explanation if you've made a mistake.
- Share the steps you have taken to resolve the issue on your own.
- Ask for help and explain how you believe the situation can be resolved. Offer specific solutions.
- End with a call to action, such as "I look forward to hearing from you soon" or "Please let me know if you have ideas on how we can resolve this together."
- If you don't get a response, follow up. School

officials are often busy and overwhelmed with numerous tasks. Just because they don't respond doesn't mean they don't care. Sometimes they just need a reminder that you need their support.

Learning to self-advocate is a skill that can be refined through persistence and perseverance. I truly believe that most people genuinely want to help. Sometimes, we just need to ask for assistance and offer solutions.

Finally, keep in mind that early colleges typically provide more support for high schoolers taking college classes than dual enrollment programs through a neighborhood school. They bring professors to their high school campuses and usually monitor students' progress more closely than high school guidance counselors or community college instructors would. Our early college had a free tutoring center available throughout the school day, and once it was determined that a student was struggling, they were required to receive tutoring until they could succeed independently. Don't hesitate to consider an early college if you feel your child isn't receiving the support they need.

To Recap:

1. Don't panic if your child struggles; many college students face similar challenges. There are numerous things you can do to help ensure their success.
2. Encourage your student to talk to the professor as soon as they start struggling. Good professors want to help and often have practical solutions, insider tips, or extra support that can make a big difference.

3. Find a tutor as soon as your child starts to struggle. Free and affordable options are available.
4. Help your student self-advocate. There is almost always a solution, but it often starts with you.
5. Consider a different dual enrollment option if your child is not getting the support they need.

Most importantly, don't give up. College classes can be challenging at times, but there are many options for support and plenty of people who want to help. Stay positive and persistent. You've got this!

CHAPTER 13:
WHEN THE HIGH SCHOOL RESISTS DUAL ENROLLMENT

While most states support dual enrollment opportunities for high school students, individual schools and districts are sometimes resistant to students taking advantage of these programs. I explore the reasons behind this resistance in my blog post *Why the Dual Enrollment Path Isn't More Widely Known* on FinishCollegeinHighSchool.com. In short, there are several factors that contribute to this reluctance.

First, dual enrollment classes are often funded with state money through the school district. The state provides school districts with per-pupil revenue (PPR), meaning they receive a specific amount of money for each public school student. When funds are allocated to community colleges for dual enrollment credits, the school district often loses that revenue.

In addition, while the district may promote dual enrollment options, individual high schools can still be resistant. In our experience, officials at our neighborhood school often pushed back due to the additional administrative work required, even though it was minimal. Karissa frequently encountered this resistance; her guidance counselor regularly complained about our nontraditional approach and the extra work it created. In some cases, administrators may also resist because they prefer to maintain control over the curriculum, something they lose when students take classes offsite.

At times, schools express concerns that students may not be academically ready for college classes. This is understandable, which is why I am committed to ensuring that parents have all the necessary knowledge and resources to support their kids' success with dual enrollment. At the same time, it's important to note that schools may also fear losing their top students. High schools value their AP, IB, and honors programs, and if top students opt for dual enrollment, it could diminish the reputation of these offerings.

Karissa experienced a lot of pushback while participating in dual enrollment at our neighborhood school. I've shared that even with a demanding course load of twelve college credits in math and science for pre-med students, her guidance counselor insisted she take three additional high school classes, a request that was both excessive and unreasonable. Unfortunately, this was not the only time the school was resistant; it honestly seemed like they fought us almost every time she needed to set her schedule for the upcoming semester. However, I should add that each time we stepped in as parents, the school backed down. Below are a few ways you can intervene when your school or district is difficult.

Dual Enrollment vs. AP and IB

When exploring early-college options, many families find that schools and districts heavily promote Advanced Placement (AP) and International Baccalaureate (IB) programs while remaining nearly silent about dual enrollment opportunities.

This emphasis on AP and IB can be misleading. While these programs can lead to college credit, the process is more challenging, credit is not guaranteed, and even when credit is awarded, students often receive less credit than the time and effort they invested.

In these programs, college credit is awarded based on performance on high-stakes exams. A single AP or IB test score determines whether a student earns credit, and even high-achieving students may receive no credit if their score falls short.

Dual enrollment works differently. Students earn college credit based on a full semester of coursework—assignments, exams, papers, and participation—not one test. In most cases, earning a C or better in a dual enrollment class will result in transferable college credit. These courses are also taught by qualified professors and often better prepare students for the pace and expectations of college-level work.

Dual Enrollment vs. AP and IB cont.

If your student is a strong test-taker and aiming for an Ivy League or highly competitive university, AP or IB may make sense. But for most families, dual enrollment offers a more reliable and practical way to earn college credit in high school, and students can earn far more college credits than they would in an AP or IB program.

For more information on AP and IB programs, see my blog post "AP and IB Are NOT the Same as Dual Enrollment" on FinishCollegeinHighSchool.com.

Be Present

When our daughters were in high school, Erik and I made it a priority for one of us to attend every dual enrollment meeting with guidance counselors or advisors. Keep in mind that these types of meetings were held only twice a year, during the registration period for the upcoming semester, and we had the option to join virtually, so it wasn't a major commitment. As a result of our involvement, the school was much more cooperative when we were present during the registration process. A few times, they unexpectedly pulled Karissa out of class without our knowledge, and in those instances, they were less flexible than when we were there. These were also the occasions when they expressed frustration about the additional workload dual enrollment created for them. Although this didn't happen often, on the rare occasions it did, we simply reached out to the school and politely requested a meeting to clarify any confusion. They always seemed to back down and reach a reasonable agreement when we were present.

Do Your Research

Take the time to look up your state and district policies regarding dual enrollment. Schools and guidance counselors often seem to impose more rules and restrictions than the official guidelines, so I regularly shared those policies and asked if they could be more flexible. For example, when our neighborhood school repeatedly told us that Karissa could only take one or two college classes, a contact at the community college informed us that other students had been allowed to take three. Based on that information, I contacted the high school to ask if they would cover the cost of three classes, and they immediately agreed. Schools may not readily provide certain information, so it's important to do your own research and ask for exceptions.

Be Polite

While there were times when working with the school was frustrating, we always tried to be polite in our interactions with them. Having been a teacher for nearly 20 years, I understood that being rude or overly demanding was not a positive way to achieve our goals. I always thanked them for their time and investment in my daughters, as well as shared that I understood that we all wanted the best thing for kids. At the same time, I was also unafraid to kindly speak up when I felt their protocols were not in the best interest of my daughters. You are your child's biggest advocate. Be polite when standing up for them but also remember that it is perfectly acceptable to expect the very best for your family.

Talk to Others

Gather as much information as you can from other people. Talk to parents whose kids are also participating in dual enrollment. Together, you can share insights and experiences to maximize the benefits of the available options. Consider creating social media groups or cohorts to connect and exchange ideas. The community college is also a great place for networking; they value dual enrollment students as a significant source of revenue. Reach out to college advisors and other representatives for suggestions on how to get high schools more on board with dual enrollment. Some of the best information I received came from others and their experiences.

Reach Out to the District or State Department of Education

If the school continues to resist, consider reaching out to the district or state department. I caution against contacting them just to complain; a better approach is to seek help. Share your goal of maximizing the benefits of dual enrollment for your family and ask for their ideas or suggestions. It's important to share your struggles and the obstacles you're facing but try to keep the communication positive. Officials are much more likely to work with you when you are respectful and constructive in your approach.

Be Open to Considering Other Options

It's perfectly acceptable to find a program that better suits your family's needs. Both of my kids eventually chose to transfer to an early college. Since the sole purpose of the early college was to help students earn as many college credits as possible, they tended to be much more flexible with the courses offered and the number of college classes students could take. While we appreciated the money saved through dual enrollment at the neighborhood school, the early college proved to be a better fit for our family.

Your state department's website will likely list various dual enrollment options. You can also contact a state dual-enrollment representative for more information. As I mentioned, community colleges value dual enrollment students and are also a great resource for additional information. Every time I contacted the dual enrollment department at the college, they were eager to provide ideas on how to maximize college credits. What matters most is finding the best option for your kids and, in turn, saving as much money as possible.

While resistance can be frustrating when working with school officials, remember that it's always possible to reach an agreement. Stay positive and remember that you are your child's biggest advocate.

To Recap:

1. High schools can resist dual enrollment for various reasons, but there are several ways you can step in and advocate for what's best for your child.
2. Be present at every dual enrollment meeting; guidance counselors and advisors are likely to be more amicable when you are in attendance.
3. Research your state and district policies on dual enrollment, and if the school resists, share these policies to encourage greater flexibility.
4. Be polite when advocating for your student; being rude or overly demanding is not an effective way to achieve your goals.
5. Build networks and gather information from others to help you find the best opportunities for your child.
6. If necessary, reach out to the district or state department and ask for ideas on how to maximize the benefits of dual enrollment for your family.
7. If all else fails, consider other options. Many states provide a variety of ways to earn college credits while in high school, and there might be a better fit for your family.

Resistance doesn't have to be a negative thing. It could simply be a sign that you need to pivot and reconsider your plan, seek support from others, or find a better option for your family. The beauty is that you know what your student needs, and you have the power and freedom to seek out and determine the path that is best for your family.

CHAPTER 14:
WHEN OTHERS DON'T UNDERSTAND YOUR DECISION ABOUT DUAL ENROLLMENT

Soon after both of my daughters started taking college classes, they chose to stop attending high school altogether and focus solely on college coursework. They even left their neighborhood school to attend high schools designed to help students earn as many college credits as possible. When they made this transition, we faced a lot of concern from others regarding our decision.

Some felt that they would miss out on the high school experience and enter a world without the typical milestones and memories associated with high school, such as prom and sports events. Others worried about their safety on a college campus and the potential negative influence of young adults with bad intentions. Additionally, some were concerned that they wouldn't be able to handle the academic rigor of a full-time college schedule.

These worries are common, so let me share what I've learned after walking through them myself.

Myth #1: My Child Will Miss Out on the High School Experience

This is one of the biggest misconceptions about dual enrollment. People assumed that my daughters would lose out on milestones like prom, graduation, or playing sports. However, in truth, they enjoyed all of those things and so much more.

My youngest, Karissa, chose to spend her senior year as a full-time college student at a fun urban campus in downtown Denver. She was ready for the next chapter and excited to participate in collegiate sports. Because she was technically enrolled in an early college high school, they covered 100% of her tuition and still offered homecoming, prom, clubs, and other activities on their high school campus. As a result, she got the best of both worlds: college academics and sports, along with all the traditional high school milestones. She truly didn't miss out on a thing.

My older daughter, Caitlyn, preferred the early college campus and took most of her classes onsite with other high-schoolers. The early college brought professors to the ninth–twelfth grade campus, and students still had access to school events and extracurriculars like dances, clubs, and student activities, allowing them to stay connected to a traditional high school experience while earning college credit. Since it was a smaller environment, Caitlyn was even appointed student council president, an opportunity she might not have had at a larger, more traditional high school.

Keep in mind that if your child participates in dual enrollment through their neighborhood school, they'll either leave campus to attend community college classes, or take college-level courses taught by professors right on their high school campus. In either case, their social life will remain largely the same, and they'll still be able to participate in all the activities their high school offers. Karissa chose this path during her first three years of high school and was actively involved in sports, journalism, and other extracurriculars right at the neighborhood school.

The bottom line is that students who participate in dual enrollment won't miss out on the high school experience. They can still enjoy all the traditional milestones—and often gain even more from the opportunity. Both of my girls would tell you they never felt deprived of the "high school experience;" they simply built their own version of it.

Myth #2: My Child Won't Be Safe on a College Campus

This is a valid concern, and I'll admit, I felt it too. Sending a sixteen- or seventeen-year-old into a college classroom with adults isn't something to take lightly. There were times when I worried about my daughters encountering older students who might not have the best intentions.

What I found, however, was reassuring. Many community college classrooms are filled with returning adults— working parents, veterans, and professionals—who are focused on finishing their education, not distracting younger students. In fact, my daughters were often "adopted" by older classmates (usually moms) who wanted to encourage and support them. Professors were also notified when high-schoolers enrolled and often kept a watchful, supportive eye on the younger students.

When Karissa became a full-time student at a college in downtown Denver, I was understandably nervous about her safety. But I was impressed by the security measures in place: regular patrols by campus police, emergency phones every 100 feet, and security escorts available at any time. She never needed to use those services, but knowing they were there gave me peace of mind. What's more, over the six years my girls spent taking college classes while still in high school, neither ever encountered an unsafe situation.

As I mentioned, it's important to note that not all dual enrollment opportunities require students to step foot on a college campus. Some districts offer online options or bring college professors into the high school, while others provide blended programs that combine all of these approaches. Families have options, so concerns about safety shouldn't be a barrier to exploring these opportunities.

Myth #3: My Child Could Never Pass a College Class

I understand why parents worry about this. College can be challenging, and not every student thrives without support. But dual enrollment doesn't mean throwing kids into the deep end without help.

As I've mentioned, Caitlyn has a seizure disorder that affects her memory. If anyone had reason to doubt their success in college, it was her. Yet, with constant support from our family, school resources, and her determination to overcome challenges, she learned to thrive in college classes.

Karissa was academically stronger, but she also needed encouragement and occasional tutoring. Over time, both girls became more independent and resilient. They graduated with above-average GPAs, stronger work habits, and the life skills needed to handle challenges far beyond the classroom.

In addition, colleges offer a wide range of support services for all types of students, including those with special needs and English-language learners. Most also provide access to writing centers, tutoring labs, and academic coaching, typically at no additional cost. In fact, community colleges are so well-equipped with support systems that nearly any student can succeed in their classes with the right guidance and effort.

Of course, it wasn't always easy. But then again, traditional high school isn't always easy either. The difference is that, through dual enrollment, the challenges helped my daughters grow in meaningful ways. They learned to advocate for themselves, manage their time, and push through difficulties—skills that will serve them for life. In the end, the rewards far outweighed the hard days, and the experience also saved us tens of thousands of dollars in college tuition.

You can learn more about these and other common myths at
FinishCollegeinHighSchool.com.

Even with these concerns explained, many people still felt the need to share their doubts. Ultimately, it was our choice, and what mattered most was what was best for our kids. Although I've never been one to care much about what others think, I do understand the pressure to conform and the influence that other parents can have on our decisions.

Looking back, I don't think other families truly understood the benefits of dual enrollment or the significant amount of money we would save. They also may not have been aware of the considerable expenses they were about to face with their kids' own college experience. As a result, their lack of awareness may have led to a bias toward traditional schooling.

The truth is that education has been evolving for decades, and today there are multiple paths kids can take to complete their education, including online schools, charter schools, trade programs, and other nontraditional options. COVID also intensified the demand for these alternatives as school closures and constant quarantines led to a noticeable decline in educational quality.

When others looked at us sideways or criticized our decision, I simply shared the benefits of dual enrollment and our reasoning for choosing this option and then moved on. I felt it was better to agree to disagree rather than spend a lot of time and energy trying to convince them we were doing what was best for our family.

What's interesting is that most of our critics later admitted they wished they had considered dual enrollment themselves, especially after seeing how much our daughters gained from the experience. Rather than missing out, they stayed active in both high school and college communities, fully engaging in academics, athletics, and leadership opportunities. Many were also amazed when both girls graduated college a week before finishing high school, and once they saw the price tag for a four-year university, they finally understood the benefits of earning some of those credits in high school.

In the end, it really wasn't worth worrying about what other people thought of our decision. The people who truly cared about us supported our journey, and we were confident that we were making the right choice. The fact that our girls will graduate college completely debt-free is all the confirmation we need.

To Recap:

1. Because so many myths exist around dual enrollment, people might not understand your decision to have your child participate, which could lead to bias in favor of traditional schooling.
2. Alternative forms of education are becoming more widespread, and choosing a different approach will gradually gain greater acceptance.
3. If others criticize your decision, simply explain the benefits of dual enrollment and then move on.
4. Once people realize that students can have a typical high school experience while saving thousands of dollars on tuition, they'll better understand why you chose that path.

5. Ultimately, what truly matters is that you have made the best choice for your family.

Dual enrollment can lead to significant savings, and in the end, those who truly care will stand behind your decision. What matters most is that you've chosen what's right for your family. Other people's opinions are just noise; they won't be there to help your kids pay off student loan debt.

CHAPTER 15:
WHAT YOU REALLY NEED TO KNOW ABOUT SCHOLARSHIPS

While it's a common belief that millions of dollars in scholarships go unclaimed every year, the reality is more nuanced. Many people have researched the number of unclaimed scholarships, and in the end, they concluded that this idea is simply not true. Researchers believe that the statement can be traced back to the 1970s and was never supported by actual evidence.

Mark Kantrowitz, a nationally recognized expert on financial aid, scholarships and student loans, states that while there are scholarships that go unclaimed, it's often because of highly restrictive eligibility requirements. These can include specific criteria like a student's height, family background, the town they live in, proficiency in a rare foreign language, or other uncommon characteristics.[8]

In addition, while the numbers vary from year to year, some estimates show that 0.1% of students receive full-ride scholarships (tuition, room and board, fees, and textbooks included), and only 1.5% receive full tuition scholarships.[9] In 2022, 2.34 million freshmen enrolled in a college or university,[10] and based on the 1.5% estimate, only about 35,000 would have received a full-tuition scholarship. If this is true, then there are not enough full-tuition scholarships for each high school valedictorian in the country. Also keep in mind that full tuition does not cover housing, textbooks, or fees, which could amount to an additional $14,000 or more per year.

A lot of schools don't even offer full scholarships, and the colleges our daughters selected were no exception. Both of our kids had high GPAs, a record of rigorous high school coursework, participated in community service, were highly involved in school activities, and demonstrated over two years of work experience. Yet neither received a significant amount of scholarship money. All things considered, they both received partial tuition scholarships from the university, as well as a private scholarship that helped with their first year of classes.

Caitlyn utilized several scholarship searches and applied for every award for which she was eligible. She spent hours each night working on private scholarship applications and essays, as well as reaching out to people who could provide letters of reference. On her applications, she noted that she had a high GPA, was a Girl Scout Gold recipient, served as student council president, started her own nonprofit organization, volunteered with breast cancer awareness, graduated with an associate degree, demonstrated more than two years of work experience, and even shared the challenges she faced as a teenager with a disability. (I share this to highlight that scholarships aren't always guaranteed, even for students who seem to do everything right.) In the end, after spending at least two hours every evening for over six months, she received one private award that was a blind competition based entirely on her essay—and we are beyond grateful for that scholarship.

I didn't feel that it was worth the time and energy for Karissa to apply for each and every opportunity. So, she only pursued academic scholarships through the university, as well as one private award that was offered by her high school. Ultimately, both girls ended up with roughly the same amount in scholarships.

This experience reinforced an important lesson: scholarships are highly competitive and not as easy to obtain as some might believe. In "How America Pays for College 2025," Sallie Mae reported that families who received scholarships reported an average of $8,004 in funding,[11] which is roughly the same amount my kids received. Compare that to $22,000, the average cost of in-state tuition, fees, room and board, and textbooks.

Sports scholarships are also extremely difficult to secure. They are highly competitive, and in reality, only 1–2% of high school athletes are fortunate enough to receive any form of athletic scholarship.[12] Even if a student receives an athletic award, it will most likely be a partial scholarship, meaning they will probably need additional financial resources to cover their college expenses.

As a result, it's crucial to explore other financial options alongside scholarships. While scholarships should be actively sought, keep in mind that you will likely need to find other funding sources to cover your student's college expenses.

To Recap:

1. The idea that millions of dollars in scholarships go unclaimed each year is simply not true.
2. Very few students receive full-ride or full-tuition scholarships, and many schools don't even offer full scholarships.
3. Private scholarships are highly competitive and difficult to obtain.
4. Only 1–2% of students earn any type of athletic scholarship, and very few receive full sports scholarships.
5. Families shouldn't depend entirely on scholarships to cover their kids' college education.

I sincerely hope your child receives full scholarships, private awards, athletic scholarships, or any other available assistance. If that happens, please reach out so we can celebrate together! At the same time, I encourage families to stay open-minded and plan realistically for their kids' financial futures. With thoughtful planning, you'll be better prepared for whatever comes your way.

CHAPTER 16:
THE DARK TRUTH ABOUT STUDENT LOANS

I've emphasized that student loans are a highly risky financial decision and should almost always be avoided. Unfortunately, millions of borrowers have learned this the hard way. Many have shared how the student loan industry has caused severe, lifelong financial burdens. Countless personal stories can be found on websites like StudentLoanJustice.org and StudentDebtCrisis.org. In this chapter, we'll examine the harsh realities of student loans and explore why they are so often more harmful than helpful.

According to podcaster and television host Mike Rowe, "Never in the history of Western civilization has a thing become more exponentially expensive faster than the cost of a four-year degree. That's fact. If that doesn't make you angry, then I don't know what [will]."

Given how dramatically tuition costs have risen, and with millions of Americans drowning in student loan debt, one critical question remains: where is all that money going? The answer lies in a system driven by three major players: universities, student loan companies, and the U.S.

The "Dream College" Trap

Too many young adults (and their parents) fall for the illusion of a "dream college." A campus might feel right, seem impressive, or carry prestige, but the decision to attend often comes with crushing debt. Entire websites are filled with heartbreaking stories of people who chose a dream school, only to end up buried under student loans and denied forgiveness later.

Here's the reality:

- The brain's prefrontal cortex (the decision-making center) isn't fully developed until a person is in their mid-twenties, which means teens need adult guidance for life-changing financial choices.
- Students can almost always find what they truly want, such as sports, social life, or a strong academic program, at an affordable college close to home.
- Graduating from a state school does not close the door to top opportunities. I personally know someone who earned their bachelor's degree at a state university and later went on to complete a master's degree at Harvard.

Our daughters achieved their goals, including collegiate sports, independence, and a great education, without chasing a "dream college." They found fulfillment, avoided debt, and prepared for their futures in smarter, more affordable ways.

For more on this topic, see my accompanying blog post "Myth: The Dream College on FinishCollegeinHighSchool.com."

Department of Education—all which profit immensely from the very borrowers they claim to serve.

College tuition continues to rise at an alarming rate. According to the Education Data Initiative, in 1963, tuition at a four-year public college was, on average, $243 per year. After adjusting for inflation, this figure would have been about $2,487 in 2024; however, today the cost of in-state tuition at a public four-year college is, on average, $9,750,[13] and this does not include room and board, books, or fees. It is also important to note that tuition prices are not regulated in the U.S. like they are in many other countries,[14] allowing institutions to keep raising costs without oversight.

In his book *The Student Loan Scam*, Alan Collinge of Student Loan Justice explains that student loan companies are highly profitable businesses that provide kickbacks to colleges.[15] As a result, schools steer students toward the lenders that provide the best financial rewards for the institution. This contrasts with all other loans, where consumers are free to shop around for the best option. Additionally, Collinge shares that loan companies also make massive amounts of money off defaulted loans. If a student experiences hardship and cannot make their loan payments, the original loan balance can rapidly double or triple due to penalties, fees, collection charges, and interest. The borrowing process is also intentionally confusing, and most students don't know who their lenders are or how much they are borrowing.

The U.S. Department of Education (DoED) is also profiting from the crisis, with loan companies and the federal government prioritized over students. Collinge argues that for every dollar the DoED reimburses lenders for defaulted loans, it recovers the entire principal amount, along with about 20% in interest and fees. Standard lending protections, such as bankruptcy and refinancing rights, have also been removed from student loans, making students the only borrowers stripped of these rights. It is also important to note the revolving door of employment between loan company executives, DoED representatives, and their families, meaning that individuals often move between these positions, creating potential conflicts of interest and blurring the lines between public policy and corporate influence.

Because the student loan industry heavily favors universities and loan companies, students must be proactive and involved in their role as consumers during the financial aid process. They should almost always avoid student loans at all costs, even if it means taking one or two classes at a time and paying as they go. Cost should be the primary consideration when choosing a four-year college; selecting an affordable school is far more important than choosing one that seems "fun."

Given the enormous financial pressures created by universities and loan companies, it's essential for students to take control of their financial futures and approach student loans with extreme caution. If a student decides to take out loans to fund their education, they should ensure that their future income and cost of living will support manageable loan payments.

It's especially important to understand that student loan borrowers do not have the same protections as other types of borrowers. Federal student loans cannot be discharged in bankruptcy, and borrowers typically cannot negotiate reduced payment amounts or settlements. This makes it nearly impossible to escape the debt, even in severe financial hardship.

While private student loans can sometimes be discharged in bankruptcy, it's extremely rare and difficult to do. To make matters worse, private loans often come with astronomical interest rates and fewer repayment protections than federal loans.

Finally, it's most important to remember that teenagers may not fully grasp the long-term risks associated with borrowing money for college. While young adults often have the best intentions, they may unintentionally make decisions that lead to financial hardship simply because they lack the perspective or experience to understand the full consequences. Because of this, it is vital for parents to stay actively engaged in every step of the financial aid process and offer persistent support as their kids navigate their financial futures.

To Recap:

1. Millions of borrowers have reported that their lives have been devastated by the student loan industry.
2. College tuition is rising rapidly and has significantly outpaced inflation, making it imperative to select an affordable college.

3. Student loan companies are highly profitable businesses that prioritize the interests of universities and their own over those of your child.

4. While the federal government claims to support student borrowers, it also profits from student loans and has stripped them of standard consumer protections.

5. Because young adults' brains are not fully developed, parents must stay actively involved in the financial aid process from the moment their kids apply for college until they graduate.

Parents, be on guard. Student loans can be devastating for young adults, often in ways they can't fully comprehend at the time. It's crucial to help your kids explore all available options for funding college and make sure they fully understand the long-term consequences before even considering student loans.

AFTERWORD

Two of the most meaningful days of my life were when my girls graduated from high school. As they walked across the stage and the principal announced their names, followed by "graduating from high school with an associate degree," I took great pride in the fact that they had accomplished something not many teenagers are able to achieve.

I also felt a great deal of joy when Caitlyn graduated from college completely debt-free. I knew that she had the freedom to pursue anything she wanted. She could work the job of her choice, even if it was low paying. She could take an internship in another state. She could travel to explore places she'd never been. Because she was beginning her young adult life without the burden of debt, she had the kind of flexibility and opportunity that many people can only dream of. I am excited for Karissa to experience the same freedom.

Since Erik and I graduated with a massive amount of debt, I never thought my kids would be able to achieve such a remarkable feat. We spent so many years unable to eat out, take vacations, or buy new things, and there were times when we weren't sure we could stretch our budget far enough to cover even our basic needs. I am so thankful for the gift of dual enrollment and for the hard work and sacrifices my kids made to ensure their financial freedom.

As parents, we all want our kids to have the best of everything, while also ensuring they don't miss out on the opportunities and experiences their peers enjoy. At times, it was hard to watch my girls struggle through a grueling college class or miss a pep rally because they were expected on the college campus. But I believe the hard work and responsibility they faced taught them far more valuable lessons than they would have learned if they had stayed solely on the high school campus. In the end, neither of them has ever regretted participating in dual enrollment; instead, they found it both rewarding and enjoyable.

Young adults face more challenges today than ever before, especially when it comes to financial stability. Many struggle to earn enough to cover their living expenses and start a family. In fact, a recent study by MassMutual found that nearly a quarter of young adults do not plan to have children, primarily due to financial reasons.[16] They also can't afford to buy a house, and with the rapidly rising cost of living, they find it hard to live comfortably on a starting salary. If we can help our kids begin their young adult lives debt-free, we can also help them begin building a future they're excited about.

Thank you for considering the road less traveled. This journey is so much more than taking college classes while in high school. It is character-building, teaching the value of hard work. It is confidence-building, showing what it means to go against the flow and follow your own path. It is relationship-building, helping young people appreciate all types of people and the richness they bring to their lives. And most importantly, taking college classes is life-changing, as they instill self-worth, determination, and a sense of empowerment. Through the struggles, challenges, celebrations, and rewards, your kids will learn that they alone have the power to create the life they want—one filled with the people, experiences, and milestones of their choosing.

You can do this, my friend. But more importantly, your kids can do this.

Now go inspire them.

ACKNOWLEDGEMENTS

To **Colorado Early Colleges**, the school that refuses to place ceilings on kids. You didn't just save our family tens of thousands of dollars in tuition—you opened doors of opportunity that will ripple for a lifetime. Grateful is far too small a word.

To **Stephanie Chandler** and the remarkable team at **Authority Publishing**—thank you for guiding me with expertise, encouragement, and patience. You turned a dream I first had in second grade into a book I now hold in my hands.

To my gifted editors and fellow warrior moms, **Natalie Tomlin** and **Amberly Finarelli**—your insight and dedication lifted this manuscript beyond what I imagined. You made me a stronger writer, and your influence is woven throughout these pages.

To **Zoe Mathers**—thank you for giving this tech-challenged Gen Xer a digital presence and the confidence to share my voice in today's online world.

To **Pamela Silsby**—your encouragement taught me to imagine bigger, to stretch farther, and to believe that I can accomplish anything.

To **Alan Collinge** and **Student Loan Justice**—your tireless decades of advocacy for those burdened by unfair debt have inspired me deeply. Thank you for being a voice for the voiceless.

To my **friends and family**—thank you for believing in me, for encouraging this book long before it existed, and for enduring my countless rants about the dangers of student loans. Your constant support made this journey possible.

To **Caitlyn and Karissa**—you have already achieved more than I ever dreamed at your age. I am beyond proud of the incredible young women you have become. You are, and always will be, my heroes.

And to **Erik**, my one and only—thank you for walking every step of this path beside me. Of all the stories I will ever tell, ours will always be my favorite.

BONUS:
WRITING WITH CONFIDENCE AT THE COLLEGE LEVEL

Many college students, including those in dual enrollment programs, often struggle with college-level writing. High schools primarily focus on preparing students for standardized tests, and as a result, they don't have the critical thinking skills necessary for collegiate writing. In addition, most high schoolers are never introduced to researched-based writing, and the rigor of writing-intensive courses—such as English, history, and the social sciences—often leaves college students feeling overwhelmed in their first semesters. While my kids performed well in their high school English classes, neither was ready for college-level writing. As a result, I needed to take specific actions to ensure their success.

Strong writing skills are foundational to academic success across all college disciplines. Students who master research-based writing demonstrate improved critical thinking, clearer communication, and higher achievement in both humanities and STEM fields.

Most schools require students to take English Composition 101 or its equivalent during their first semester of college, and a good English professor will utilize the course to prepare students for academic writing. My daughters' English 101 instructors spent the entire fifteen weeks walking them through the process of writing an eight-to-twelve-page college-level research paper. The assignment was divided into sections, starting with the title page and extending through the introduction, thesis statement, position on the topic, supporting details, consideration of opposing arguments, conclusion, and references—all adhering to a specific citation style (APA, MLA, etc.). This allowed the students to focus on a portion of the paper each week and gradually complete it throughout the semester. It also allowed the professor to provide regular feedback and support while students were completing the assignment.

I can't emphasize enough the importance of choosing a good professor. Instructors sometimes complicate writing assignments beyond necessity, offer ineffective feedback, struggle to guide students through the writing process, or grade more harshly than necessary. When students are learning collegiate writing, they need a professor who fosters a supportive learning environment and can guide them through the writing process with clarity.

While my daughters had good English professors who provided a lot of in-class support, I still felt that they needed additional guidance and scaffolding. As a former high-school English teacher, I was able to step in and help with the writing process, including organizing the paper, writing a draft, and editing the final version. However, if you don't feel comfortable providing this level of one-on-one support, most colleges provide free writing centers or tutoring services as an alternative.

When paired with direct instruction from a professor, guided support from a parent or tutor can set students up for success with all future college writing endeavors. This bonus chapter will help you provide the guidance your student needs to approach college writing with greater confidence and clarity, supporting them through every step of writing an effective college paper.

Help Your Child Get a Clear Understanding of the Assignment

We always began by carefully reviewing the paper requirements to understand exactly what the professor expected. Did the assignment call for a well-argued thesis supported by evidence, reasoning, and counterpoints? Was it a research paper requiring documentation, historical context, or data? Or was it a reflection or a conversational post for a discussion board? Whatever the format, it's essential to start by making sure the student fully understands the assignment.

Assist in Choosing a Topic

It is most important for your child to choose a topic that interests them. Our youngest, Karissa, hates to write. She prefers a math/science class over English or social sciences any day of the year. When she was required to write papers, it was imperative that we helped her select topics that she found interesting. I knew that if she was not engaged in the topic, she would really struggle with the assignment. Since she is a dancer, she often chose subject matter involving body image and athletes. For a history class, she wrote about society's ideal female body and how it has evolved over the decades. For physics, she wrote about Newton's laws of motion and how they affect a dancer's capabilities. She would never say that she enjoyed writing any of these papers, but because she was interested in the topics, she was at least able to find the stamina to persevere and finish the assignments. Guiding your student toward choosing the right focus for a paper is the most important thing you can do to help them with writing.

Map Out the Paper Together

Many professors will require students to create an outline prior to starting the paper. While we completed one when necessary, unless the professor required it, we didn't usually worry about drafting a perfectly structured outline. However, we did always start with a framework for the assignment.

Below are steps for your child to consider when mapping out the paper.

- Based on the requirements of the paper: What argument are you trying to make, or what do you want to inform the reader about?
- What are three or four ideas that support this argument or provide more information on the topic? Make sure these main ideas will be able to generate enough research and reflection to meet the page requirements of the paper.
- If you are writing an argumentative paper, what are some opposing thoughts or disagreements to

your position? (An AI assistant like ChatGPT is a good tool for finding opposing arguments to your position.)

- How can you conclude the paper? For instance, you could restate your thesis and main points, and finish by emphasizing what you want the reader to know.

The professor may specify other ideas to include, such as additional background information on the topic, or they might want students to propose a solution, so make sure to consider any additional requirements as you are helping your child map out the assignment. Keep in mind that the paper will evolve as they write. The initial framework is not concrete, so they can feel free to add additional ideas, research, and even adjust their position as they write.

Assist in Conducting the Research

Professors typically expect a certain number of sources; in most cases, two or three must be scholarly, while the rest can be popular sources like news articles or websites. For the scholarly source requirement, they will typically need to find peer-reviewed studies in academic journals, and the college usually provides an online database like ERIC or Google Scholar for this purpose. They will need to search using targeted keywords and then apply filters in the database to limit results to peer-reviewed, full-text journal articles. Once they identify a relevant academic study, they can also consult its reference list to discover additional related research.

Once my kids found the required number of academic sources, I then encouraged them to turn to popular or general-interest sources for all of the remaining research. My daughters felt that news and magazine articles, websites, social media, podcasts, and other less-formal resources were easier to understand, more engaging, and could easily be found through a quick Google search. Just now, I simply Googled "Article on how the ideal female body has changed over time," and posts from *CNN, The American Medical Association, HuffPost, The Daily Mail, Health Digest, The Metropolitan Museum of Art*, and many others instantly appeared.

It's important to remember that even though popular sources can add color and context, academic sources must still be cited within the paper at least once, unless otherwise specified by the professor.

Once your kids find a resource they like, they should start compiling a document with the title, URL and a brief sentence describing the content. They don't need to use all of the sources they find, but they will want to have them available as they write. There were many times when we started writing and wished that we had saved a particular article, so I recommend noting everything, even if you don't think you'll use it. Don't overcomplicate the search for sources; simply Google the topic and main points and start documenting.

Once your child finds multiple sources, they should be able to frame them around the points in the outline. Your student should not feel like they need to research for hours.

They should just do a few Google searches to find enough sources to support their outline/framework. If need be, they can always find more sources once they start writing. The internet is full of information, so your child will be able to find more sources as they come up with new perspectives on the paper. Remind them that it is most important that they find the minimum required sources and properly cite them in the specified citation style. It is extremely frustrating to work tirelessly on a paper only to have your grade reduced due to insufficient references or incorrect citations.

Encourage Your Child to Get Started

"Do it messy. Do it scared. Do it anyway. Like Nike says, 'Just do it.' There's this idea that everything needs to feel perfect and polished before you take the first or next step.... And that mentality will keep you stuck and waiting for way too long.... sometimes your whole life."—Dean Graziosi

Often the hardest part of writing a paper is getting the first words on a page. Students often think that it should be perfectly planned out and completely developed before they begin. This could not be further from the truth. Instead, encourage your child to just start writing. Even if the grammar is less than perfect and ideas are still taking shape, their thoughts will evolve and improve as they engage in the process.

I do not recommend starting with the introduction; the opening is much easier to add after most of the paper is written. Instead, I suggest beginning with the thesis statement, which should be clear, assertive, and focused while confidently conveying the central message of the paper. Unless specified otherwise, it should avoid first-person language, excessive emotional tone, preachiness, or exaggeration. Do not let your student overthink the thesis statement. Simply consider the instructor's requirements for the paper, along with the message they wish to convey, and help them sum it up in one or two sentences.

Example Thesis Statements

Assignment: The English professor assigned a six-to-eight-page paper exploring a cultural issue, analyzing its societal impacts, and proposing solutions.

Thesis Statement: This paper will examine the effects of the media on body image and address several concerning organizations that misrepresent the female body; it will also offer solutions to promote positive thinking and healthy living.

Assignment: The history professor assigned an eight-to-ten-page paper exploring the historical impact of a major event or issue, including key developments, influential figures, and broader societal responses.

Thesis Statement: This paper will review the AIDS epidemic from the early 1980s to today, providing a historical timeline of the disease, while acknowledging the government's involvement in the outbreak. It will also examine scientific study and breakthroughs surrounding the disease, as well as significant people who played a role in the history of the epidemic.

Assignment: The science professor assigned a six-to-eight-page opinion paper that analyzes a natural disaster and weighs the pros and cons of living in a disaster-prone area.

Thesis Statement: In this paper, I will explore the pros and cons to living in an area prone to hurricanes. I will also share my opinion regarding this issue.

While your child can always modify their thesis statement, this concise plan, summarized in one or two sentences, serves as a blueprint for the entire paper. The thesis should guide them as they write, providing a clear path through each section of the paper and helping maintain focus on the topic and supporting points.

Guide Your Child in Writing the Paper

When my kids wrote their first college papers, I assumed the role of a tutor and walked them through the process. We created a shared Google Doc and wrote the paper together. I helped them organize their sources and fit them into the appropriate places in the paper, much like completing a jigsaw puzzle.

Some students may not require this level of support, but I was particularly motivated for my kids to gain a clear understanding of the writing process. I believed that this foundation would instill confidence in handling future writing assignments. Many young people drop out of college because they feel overwhelmed or discouraged by writing. I didn't want my kids to feel unprepared or without the tools to succeed in college-level writing.

We usually completed the paper over a series of days or even weeks, and I never allowed them to wait until the last minute and cram hours of work into one or two evenings. At the time, they were busy with afterschool activities, worked part time jobs, and also had other homework demands, so we actively scheduled time on the calendar to work on the paper. We usually set a goal to complete one to three pages per night. This approach broke the assignment into manageable pieces, reducing any feelings of overwhelm or stress. In addition, it taught them time management, as well as the importance of avoiding procrastination.

While writing, your child should always make a conscious effort to avoid plagiarism. Professors utilize various tools to confirm the originality of students' work and to identify potential plagiarism. This includes running the assignment through plagiarism detection software, conducting Google searches, as well as other methods.

You can share the following guidelines with your child to help them safeguard against committing plagiarism.

- Cite Everything! When using someone else's words, ideas, or information, provide proper citations. Always. No matter what. For more information on how to cite your sources, see the Citations section later in this chapter.
- Paraphrase Properly: When pulling information from your sources, make sure to rephrase it in your own words. Keep in mind that even though you are paraphrasing, you still need to provide a citation.

- Quote Properly: If you copy something from a source word-for-word, make sure to use quotation marks and a proper citation.
- Check Your Paper with Plagiarism Detection Software: This can help uncover unintentional plagiarism and reveal where you may need additional citations or proper paraphrasing. You can find free plagiarism checkers online.

Remember, your child is writing a rough draft, so the paper does not need to be perfect. They will go back to edit and revise later. They should just get it done. Students often hate writing because they spend too much time staring at a screen and trying to get it perfect. Any professional writer will tell you that it will never be perfect. That's why there are the sixth, seventh, and eighth editions of best sellers. Good professors are not concerned about perfection. They just want to see that students can effectively present information, critically think, and support their ideas with research.

Writing can feel overwhelming, but I am confident that your child can do it. Schedule small blocks of time to do the work. Knock out a few pages a day. And the draft will be done in no time.

Teach Your Child How to Use AI Writing Tools Appropriately

More and more students are using tools like ChatGPT, Grammarly, or other AI-based apps to help with college-level writing, and that's okay, as long as they use them responsibly. AI can be very helpful with brainstorming, outlining, checking grammar, or sentence structure. However, it is also important for students to understand the limits of these tools and the potential risks of misuse. If your child chooses to use AI during the writing process, remind them that it should be used as a writing assistant, not a replacement for their own thinking. They should think of AI as a tutor and not a shortcut to avoid doing the work. Just like a calculator in math, AI can be a powerful support, but it's still your child who needs to do the thinking. Below are appropriate uses of AI:

- Brainstorming or narrowing down a writing topic
- Organizing an outline or structuring ideas
- Rephrasing or improving awkward sentences
- Checking grammar, spelling, or punctuation
- Learning citation formats (MLA, APA, etc.)
- Asking for clarification on confusing topics
- Practicing how to paraphrase or summarize properly
- Generating sample thesis statements for comparison

Below are inappropriate uses of AI:

- Copying and pasting AI-generated content and submitting it as original work
- Relying on AI to write entire paragraphs or full papers
- Using fake sources or citations created by AI without verifying them
- Skipping reading or research and depending on AI to fill in the gaps
- Submitting assignments without understanding the content

- Violating the school's academic honesty or plagiarism policies

As AI use becomes more widespread, many colleges and universities are developing clear policies around when and how these tools may be used. Some professors encourage AI for help with writing drafts or grammar support, while others may restrict its use entirely. These expectations can vary by course, department, or institution. That's why students should always check the class syllabus or ask the professor directly before using AI on an assignment. Even unintentional misuse could result in academic consequences.

Help Your Child Write the Introduction

After they write the draft, have your child go back and write the introduction. They won't believe how much easier it will be to write the intro paragraph after drafting the paper. Remember, the opening paragraph does not need to be lengthy or exhaustive. Instead, it should grab the reader's attention, state the argument or point, and inform on how the writer will support their stance.

Start the introduction with a compelling statement, question, quote, anecdote, or relevant fact to engage the reader. While conducting research and writing the body of the draft, your child will often come across a quote, fact, or story that serves as an effective attention-grabber. Take note of this so that it's readily available when they are ready to start the introduction.

Follow the attention-grabber with one or more sentences that naturally connect it to the thesis statement. The goal is to smoothly lead into the thesis statement by providing the reader with background information or supporting details to enhance your stance on the topic. The thesis is usually the last sentence in the introduction.

Example Introductions

The Media's Influence on Body Image: How Unrealistic Beauty Standards Fuel Self-Image Issues

"I was a size 0 when a modeling agency labeled me plus size.... With the average U.S. woman wearing a size 16 to 18, that is purely ludicrous. I had lots of interest from agents, but my size always turned them off—they didn't know what to do with me.... Even at a size 2, I had multiple agents turn me down and encourage me to shave inches off my hips.... It's disheartening when I meet people who think of me as bigger—I am a size 4" (Gould).[17]

For years, the media has inaccurately portrayed the female body, promoting a standard of beauty that is both unrealistic and unhealthy. As a result, many individuals develop negative self-image and may struggle with eating disorders (Smith).[18] This paper will examine the effects of the media on body image and address several concerning organizations that misrepresent the female body; it will also offer solutions to promote positive thinking and healthy living.

HIV/AIDS in Historical Perspective: Government Responses, Research Milestones, and the People Who Shaped the Epidemic

Many celebrities, including Freddie Mercury, Magic Johnson, and Charlie Sheen, have had the courage to publicly acknowledge their HIV status in order to help and educate others. Jonathan Van Ness, from Netflix's popular series *Queer Eye*, recently released a memoir in which he revealed that he is HIV positive. He is actively working to reduce the stigma and misconceptions surrounding those living with HIV. Van Ness proudly describes himself as a "member of the beautiful HIV-positive community." (Hawgood).[19] While Van Ness and other celebrities have the freedom and acceptance from society to openly share their HIV status, this has not always been possible.

This paper will review the AIDS epidemic from the early 1980s to today, providing a historical timeline of the disease, while acknowledging the government's involvement in the outbreak. It will also examine scientific study and breakthroughs surrounding the disease, as well as significant people who played a role in the history of the epidemic (Hawgood).[19]

Assessing Risk and Reward: Should People Choose to Live in Hurricane-Prone Regions?

Should humans voluntarily live in an area that is subject to hurricanes? There are various opinions on this topic. In this paper, I will explore the pros and cons to living in an area prone to hurricanes. I will also share my opinion regarding this issue.

Now that you've seen some examples, keep this in mind: Your child is still in the draft stages of their writing. Don't let them overthink the introduction or make it more difficult than it needs to be. They should just begin with a compelling attention-grabber, conclude with the thesis statement, and connect the two with one or more sentences that support their stance.

Help Them Write the Conclusion

Since the conclusion should tie back to the introduction, it often helps to write it immediately after drafting the introductory paragraph to maintain a strong connection between the two. The concluding paragraph should include the following:

- A restating of the thesis. Avoid simply copying and pasting. Rephrasing it adds a fresh perspective and makes the writing more appealing.
- A summary of the main points or arguments to help the reader remember the key ideas.
- If the paper presented a problem, a resolution should be offered to provide a sense of closure.

- A highlighting of the significance of the stance, why it matters to the reader, and, if applicable, encouragement for continued exploration and ongoing discussion of the topic.
- A memorable closing statement. This could be a thought-provoking remark, call to action, quote, or final reflection. Your child could also refer back to the attention-grabber in the introduction to create a sense of completeness and circularity.

Similar to what I advised for the introduction, keep the conclusion straightforward and avoid overthinking it. Your child will have time to go back and edit later. Just make sure they restate the thesis, summarize the main points, and finish with a memorable remark. This will create a concise ending and leave a lasting impression on the reader.

Example Conclusion 1:

We must continue working to combat the harmful messages sent by the media and influential organizations such as Victoria's Secret, Disney, and Mattel. For centuries, society has inaccurately portrayed the female body, promoting a narrow and unrealistic standard of beauty. These distorted ideals have led to negative self-image, unattainable expectations, and unhealthy behaviors, including eating disorders. These toxic standards must end. It's time for women to reject society's toxic definitions of beauty and embrace self-acceptance.

Oprah Winfrey, a powerful voice for body positivity and self-love, once said: "Step away from the mean girls and say bye-bye to feeling bad about your looks. Are you ready to stop colluding with a culture that makes so many of us feel physically inadequate? Say goodbye to your inner critic, and take this pledge to be kinder to yourself and others."

Example Conclusion 2:

While we have come a long way in addressing HIV, there is still much to be done. Scientists continue working tirelessly toward a cure, and we all have a role to play by reducing the stigma and discrimination that still surround the disease. In the early 1980s, misinformation and fear shaped public understanding, often fueled by a lack of government response and support. Since then, medical breakthroughs have dramatically improved the lives of those living with HIV, thanks to the efforts of countless researchers, activists, and advocates. It's essential that we remember the long, painful journey, including those who lost their lives, and honor the many individuals who fought for awareness, funding, and compassion. By continuing to educate ourselves and support scientific progress, we move closer to a permanent solution. Many lives still depend on it (Soller).[20]

Example Conclusion 3:

In conclusion, hurricanes are serious and potentially deadly storms. While there are certainly drawbacks to living in hurricane-prone areas, including high costs, strict regulations, lack of privacy, and the threat of destruction or injury, I believe the benefits outweigh the risks. Beach homes can provide a valuable source of income and significantly enhance both physical and mental well-being. Additionally, the likelihood of dying in a hurricane is extremely low. Ultimately, people should have the freedom to choose where they live, even if it involves risk. We shouldn't let fear dictate our lives.

Assist With Citations

Most professors will require correct citations throughout the paper, followed by a final page with references. There are various citation styles including APA (American Psychological Association), MLA (Modern Language Association), Chicago, Harvard, and others. Each style has its own set of rules regarding how to format citations for various sources including books, articles, websites, etc.

Each professor will usually indicate which citation style they require, and there are guides and manuals available that inform on how to cite different sources, as well as create the final references page. Your child can also find information about citation styles by visiting the college writing or tutoring center, as well as by conducting an internet search.

It is also important that your child documents as they go. Help them make it a habit to record citation details (website URL, author, title, publication information, etc.) as they gather information during their research. This will save time when they're ready to compile the bibliography. Also make sure they cite within the text as they write the draft. It is extremely time-consuming to have to go back and attempt to remember which sources were referenced after the paper is written.

There are also several online tools and platforms like EasyBib.com, and even ChatGPT, that help with formatting bibliographies and managing citations. These platforms have generators that create citations in the various styles and also provide resources on how to cite different sources.

In my opinion, Microsoft Word offers the most user-friendly method for generating citations. From the References tab in Word, your child can easily cite sources in the various styles. They start by selecting the citation style, and then input all necessary details into the generator, including author, title, publication year, etc. As they write the paper, whenever they need to cite a source, they can just click on "insert citation," and all of their sources will automatically populate. From there, they can select the specific source they wish to cite, and Word will seamlessly generate the citation, embedding it directly into the paper.

When they're ready to create the final reference page, they can navigate to "Bibliography" under the "References" tab. Choose the desired citation style format, such as References, Works Cited, or Bibliography, and Word will automatically generate the final reference page. Microsoft's citation feature allows students to effortlessly cite sources within seconds. It's important to note that some professors may mandate the use of the latest edition of a citation style, such as MLA Edition 9. If your Word software isn't the most recent version, it may not generate citations in the latest edition of the citation style. If this is the case, your child will need to update their citations to align with the most current edition.

Finally, if your child is new to college-level writing, I highly recommend they visit the school's writing center or schedule a meeting with the professor during office hours to verify the accuracy of their citations. While many professors are not overly stringent about references, there are some who can be meticulous, and your child wouldn't want their grade to be affected by a technical error.

While citing references can feel tedious, citations are an integral part of academic writing, as they help students understand the importance of honesty, credibility, and the responsible use of information. Documenting as they go, utilizing online tools and generators, and receiving feedback from a professor or writing center will help ensure the accuracy of the citations and streamline the overall process.

Oversee the Editing Process

After drafting the paper, including the introduction with thesis, body with main points, conclusion, and reference page, revisiting and editing the writing will be necessary. First, make sure the paper is the minimum required number of pages; if it falls short, your child will need to go back and add more content.

Some students feel comfortable editing their own work, but many need outside support. There are several online editing tools that can help with corrections and feedback on college papers. While many of them provide free versions, some also offer premium upgrades with additional features and capabilities. Many of these platforms not only assess grammar, spelling, punctuation, and plagiarism but also offer recommendations for enhancing clarity and style.

Earlier today, I explored Grammarly for the first time. I registered for a free account, processed a seven-and-a-half-page paper through the editing software, and implemented the recommended edits—all in under ten minutes. Most of the recommendations were accurate, but as is common with all AI technology, there were also mistakes. Therefore, please don't assume that your child can rely entirely on an online editor.

I recommend all students get a human to review the paper as well. Your child can ask for guidance from the professor during office hours, visit the college writing or tutoring center, or have someone they know who has a knack for writing offer suggestions.

Professors understand that everyone makes occasional mistakes, but submitting papers with a high number of errors often leads them to believe that the student doesn't care about the quality of their work. Although I don't think the editing process should be excessively stressful or time-consuming, I do encourage students to make use of available resources to improve the quality of their work. Professors will recognize and consider this effort when assigning grades for both the paper and the class.

Encourage Your Child to Get Feedback and Make Revisions

I mentioned the importance of students visiting the college's writing center and/or meeting with the professor during office hours to receive feedback on their work in progress. This will ensure that they correctly understand the assignment's requirements and submit a well-executed paper. In addition, during a student's first college English class, the professor typically assigns a substantial paper to be completed throughout the semester, with various sections submitted gradually. This allows them to provide regular feedback to ensure that the student is completing the assignment correctly and making revisions as needed.

When your child receives feedback in any format, make sure that they heed the advice and make the recommended revisions. It may seem silly that I suggest this, but as a high school English teacher, I was always shocked at the number of students who disregarded my edits and suggestions and turned in their essays without any revisions. This lack of effort typically resulted in a deduction of one or more letter grades and led me to assume that they didn't take their studies seriously. In college, professors have very little patience for such apathetic behaviors.

In addition, if a student incorporates all of the professor's recommended revisions and the instructor provides a less-than-favorable final grade, the student can appeal it. Our oldest, Caitlyn, experienced this. She completed a lengthy paper and submitted the draft to her professor for review. After receiving feedback and making the recommended revisions, Caitlyn was disappointed to find her final grade was a C. Consequently, she appealed to her professor, highlighting her adherence to the suggested revisions, and inquired about the absence of additional requirements in the initial feedback. As a result, the professor agreed to reassess the paper and eventually awarded a higher grade.

Manage the Final Touches

Once the paper is in its final draft, help your child make sure it is formatted correctly with any necessary elements, including a title page, page numbers, headers, abstract, correct citations, reference page, etc. Finally, remind them to make any last-minute edits and ensure that the paper is turned in on time.

Now it is time to celebrate! Rest assured that with experience, writing will become easier. While significant support may be needed in those initial courses, parents can usually step back as students gain confidence. And remember, if you don't feel comfortable helping, there are many other supports available to ensure your child's success.

Finally, don't get discouraged if your high-schooler struggles with college-level writing. Some studies show that nearly three-fourths of twelfth-graders lack writing proficiency.[21] Good professors understand this and offer support when needed. Even the best writers know that improvement comes through practice and persistence. Remind your child that their first paper will likely be their worst, and that their skills will improve with time and experience. Writing also becomes easier with each class. And if they're like Karissa and really dislike writing, they can choose a less writing-intensive major.

Writing doesn't have to be the reason students feel unsuccessful in college. In fact, dual enrollment offers a great opportunity to build writing skills in a supportive setting, giving students space to grow before facing the full weight of college expectations. With the right support and mindset, every student can grow into a clear, confident writer—regardless of where they are in their writing journey.

NOTES

1. Melanie Hanson, "Student Loan Debt Statistics [2025]: Average + Total Debt," EducationData.org, last modified August 8, 2025, https://educationdata.org/student-loan-debt-statistics.
2. Erik L. Hernandez and Christopher Mazur, "Homeownership by Young Households Below Pre-Great Recession Levels," U.S. Census Bureau, November 17, 2022, https://www.census.gov/library/stories/2022/11/homeownership-by-young-households-below-pre-great-recession-levels.html.
3. Lawrence Mishel, Elise Gould, and Josh Bivens, "Wage Stagnation in Nine Charts," Economic Policy Institute, January 6, 2015, https://www.epi.org/publication/charting-wage-stagnation/.
4. Alan Collinge, The Student Loan Scam: The Most Oppressive Debt in U.S. History, and How We Can Fight Back (Beacon, Enfield, 2010).
5. Collinge, The Student Loan Scam.
6. Tatiana Velasco, John Fink, Mariel Bedoya-Guevara, and Davis Jenkins, "The Postsecondary Outcomes of High School Dual Enrollment Students: A National and State-by-State Analysis" (New York: Community College Research Center, Teachers College, Columbia University, October 2024), https://ccrc.tc.columbia.edu/

publications/postsecondary-outcomes-dual-enrollment-national-state.html.

7. "College Dropout Rates: 2025 Statistics by Race, Gender & Income," Research.com, accessed October 19, 2025, https://research.com/universities-colleges/college-dropout-rates.

8. Mark Kantrowitz, "Do Scholarships Ever Go Unclaimed?" SavingForCollege.com, updated July 14, 2020, https://www.savingforcollege.com/article/do-scholarships-ever-go-unclaimed.

9. Imed Bouchrika, "72 Scholarship Statistics: 2025 Data, Facts & Analysis," Research.com, accessed October 19, 2025, https://research.com/research/scholarship-statistics.

10. Johanna Alonso, "Freshman Enrollment Is Up for the First Time Since 2019," Inside Higher Ed, February 1, 2023, https://www.insidehighered.com/news/institutions/community-colleges/2023/02/01/freshman-enrollment-first-time-2019.

11. "How America Pays for College 2025," Sallie Makes Sense, September 4, 2025, https://salliemakessense.com/how-america-pays-for-college-2025/.

12. Signature College Counseling, "What Percent of College Athletes Get Full Ride Scholarships?" SignatureCollegeCounseling.com, accessed October 19, 2025, https://www.signaturecollegecounseling.com/what-percent-of-college-athletes-get-full-ride-scholarships/.

13. Imed Bouchrika, "College Tuition Inflation [2025]: Rate Increase Statistics," EducationData.org, accessed October 19, 2025, https://educationdata.org/college-tuition-inflation-rate.

14. Jessica Bryant and John Boitnott, "Why Is College So Expensive? 5 Reasons," BestColleges, May 7, 2025, https://www.bestcolleges.com/news/analysis/why-is-college-so-expensive/.

15. Collinge, The Student Loan Scam.

16. MassMutual, "MassMutual Consumer Spending and Saving Index: Many Americans Are Opting for Childfree Lives," September 2024, https://www.massmutual.com/about-us/news-and-press-releases/press-releases/2024/09/massmutual-consumer-spending-and-saving-index-many-americans-are-opting-for-childfree-lives?ftag=MSFd61514f.

17. Gould, Hallie. "I Was a Size 0 When a Modeling Agency Labeled Me 'Plus Size.'" Byrdie. March 31, 2019.

18. Smith, Sarah. "The Media's Portrayal of the Human Body Are Totally Inaccurate and Unrealistic." The Odyssey Online, December 26, 2017. https://www.theodysseyonline.com/medias-portrayal-human-body-totally-inaccurate-unrealistic.

19. Hawgood, Alex. "Jonathan Van Ness of 'Queer Eye' Comes Out." The New York Times, September 21, 2019.

20. Soller, Kurt, ed. "Six Times Journalists on the Paper's History of Covering AIDS and Gay Issues." T Magazine, The New York Times, April 27, 2018. https://www.nytimes.com/2018/04/27/t-magazine/times-journalists-aids-gay-history.html.

21. Dana Goldstein, "Why Kids Can't Write," The New York Times, August 2, 2017, https://www.nytimes.com/2017/08/02/education/edlife/writing-education-grammar-students-children.html.

www.ingramcontent.com/pod-product-compliance
Lightning Source LLC
Chambersburg PA
CBHW060530130626
46553CB00002B/701